westermann

W0307976

EinFach Englisch

YOUNG ADULT LITERATURE

Series Editor:
Iris Edelbrock

Jennifer Clement

Gun Love

Edited by
Iris Edelbrock

Sprachliche Betreuung: John Poziemski

Druck A[3] / Jahr 2024
Alle Drucke der Serie A sind im Unterricht parallel verwendbar.

Redaktion: Marion Kramer
Umschlaggestaltung: LIO Design; Foto: Renars Pranevskis/Alamy Stock Photo
Druck und Bindung: Westermann Druck GmbH, Georg-Westermann-Allee 66, 38104 Braunschweig

ISBN 978-3-14-**127470**-7

Contents

For Barbara

Part One

1

My mother was a cup of sugar. You could borrow her anytime. My mother was so sweet, her hands were always birthday-party sticky. Her breath held the five flavors of Life Savers candy. And she knew all the love songs that are a university for love. She knew 'Slowly Walk Close to Me,' 'Where Did You Sleep Last Night?,' 'Born Under A Bad Sign,' and all the I'll-kill-you-if-you-leave-me songs.

But sweetness is always looking for Mr. Bad and Mr. Bad can pick out Miss Sweet in any crowd.

My mother opened her mouth in a great wide *O* and breathed him right into her body.

I couldn't understand. She knew all the songs, so why would she get messed and stirred up with this man?

When he said his name was Eli she was down on her knees.

His voice tamed her immediately. The first words he said were all she needed. He spoke, singing, *I am your medicine sweet baby my oh me your name has always been written on my heart.*

And from there on all he had to do was whistle for her.

to borrow sb. *jdn. ausleihen*

sticky *klebrig*

Life Savers American ring-shaped candy

university here: a source of information (about love)

to get messed with sb. (*phr. v.*) to get involved with sb.

to get stirred up with sb. to get moved/excited by sb.

to tame sb. to gain control over sb.; *jdn. zähmen*

to whistle for sb. to summon sb.; *jdn. rumkommandieren, nach seiner Pfeife tanzen lassen*

2

Me? I was raised in a car and, when you live in a car, you're not worried about storms and lightning, you're afraid of a tow truck. My mother and I moved into the Mercury when she was seventeen and I was newborn. So our car, at the edge of a trailer park in the middle of Florida, was the only home I ever knew. We lived a dot-to-dot life, never thinking too much about the future.

The old car had been bought for my mother on her sixteenth birthday.

The 1994 Mercury Topaz automatic had once been red but was now covered in several coats of white from my mother painting the car every few years as if it were a house. The red paint still appeared under scratches and scrapes. Out the front window was a view of the trailer park and a large sign that read: WELCOME TO INDIAN WATERS TRAILER PARK.

Our car was turned off under a sign that said Visitors Parking. My mother thought we'd only be there for a month or two, but we stopped there for fourteen years.

Once in a while when people asked my mother what it was like to live in a car, she answered, You're always looking for a shower. The only thing we ever really worried about was CPS, Child Protective Services, coming around. My mother was afraid that someone at my school or her job might think they should call the abuse hotline on her and take me off to a foster home.

She knew the acronyms that were like the rest-in-peace letters on tombstones: CPSL, Child Protective Services Law; FCP, Foster Care Plus; and FF, Family Finding.

We can't go around making too many friends, my mother said. There's always some person who wants to be a saint and sit on a chair in heaven. A friend can become Your Honor in an instant. Since when is living in a car something you can call abuse? she asked without expecting me to answer.

The park was located in Putnam County. The land had been cleared to hold at least fifteen trailers, but there were only four trailers that were occupied. My friend April May lived in one with her parents, Rose and Sergeant Bob. Pastor Rex inhabited one all by himself while Mrs. Roberta Young and her adult daughter Noelle occupied one right next to the dilapidated recreation area. A Mexican couple, Corazón and Ray, lived in a trailer toward the back of the park, far from the entrance and our car.

We were not in the south of Florida near the warm beaches and the Gulf of Mexico. We were not near the orange groves or close to St Augustine, the oldest city in America. We were not near the Everglades, where clouds of mosquitos and a thick canopy of

tow truck *Abschleppwagen*
Mercury a compact premium car brand, produced by the Ford Motor company; defunct in 2011
edge the outer point of sth.
trailer park an area where big caravans can be parked, especially by people using them as their homes
a dot-to-dot life life like in a picture puzzle where the full image is gradually completed by combining dots
coat here: a layer; *dünne Schicht*
Child Protective Services US government agency responsible for the protection and care of children
foster home *Pflegefamilie*
Family Finding national US organization helping to connect children with a family
Your Honor (*fml.*) title of respect when speaking to a judge; *Euer Ehren!*
Putnam County county in northeastern Florida
dilapidated old and in poor condition
recreation area area to relax and enjoy yourself in
orange grove *Orangenhain*
Everglades US national park; a network of wetlands and forests
canopy *Baldachin*

vines protected delicate orchids. Miami, with its sounds of Cuban music and streets filled with convertibles, was a long drive. Animal Kingdom and the Magic Kingdom were miles away. We were nowhere.

Two highways and a creek, which we all called a river but was only a small stream off the St John's, surrounded the trailer park. The town dump was at the back through some trees. We breathed in the garbage. We breathed in gas of rot and rust, corroded batteries, decomposing food, deadly hospital waste, odors of medicines and clouds of cleaning chemicals.

My mother said, Who would clear land for a trailer park and a garbage dump on a sacred Indian ground? This land belongs to the Timucua tribes and their spirits are everywhere. If you plant a seed, something else grows. If you plant a rose, a carnation comes out of the ground. If you plant a lemon tree, this earth will give you a palm tree. If you plant a white oak, a tall man will grow. The ground here is puzzled.

My mother was right. In our part of Florida everything was puzzled. Life was always like shoes on the wrong foot.

When I read over the headlines on the newspapers that were lined up at the checkout counter at the local store beside the gum and candy, I knew Florida was asking for something. I read: DON'T CALL 911 BUY A GUN; BEAR RETURNS TO CITY AFTER BEING RELOCATED; DEADLY MEXICAN HEROIN KILLS FOUR; and HURRICANE BECOMES A CLOUDY DAY.

One summer, conjoined twin alligators appeared near our river. They had four legs and two heads.

It was my friend April May who found them. She'd been down by the river when she saw the baby alligators in the sandy earth beside the short wood dock. They still had white pieces of eggshell on the green, scaly back they shared.

April May didn't stick around. She knew what we all knew: if there's an alligator egg, then there's an angry mother alligator nearby.

That afternoon, after word had spread through the park, everyone went down to the river to see if the babies were still there. Tiny specs of white eggshells lay broken around the alligators, as the creatures had not moved from the very place they'd been born, and no mother alligator ever appeared. The babies were only a little larger than a chick.

The next morning, the first local journalists began to arrive. By the afternoon, reporters from national television stations in trucks with filming equipment had moved in. Before dusk, someone had tied one of the creatures' four legs to a palm tree with a thin blue sewing thread so that it could not escape.

orchid *Orchidee*

convertible *Cabrio*

Animal Kingdom, Magic Kingdom two theme parks at the Walt Disney World Resort in Bay Lake, Florida, near Orlando

creek (*US*), **stream** a narrow river

dump *Mülldeponie*

garbage anything people throw away, waste

rot decay; *Verwesung*

corroded eaten away by rust

decomposing breaking down into elements

odor a bad smell

to clear land to remove trees, bushes, etc. from an area

carnation *Nelke*

puzzled confused

911 the phone number used in the US to call emergency services

conjoined twins a pair of twins who were born with some part of their bodies joined together; *Siamesische Zwillinge*

dock *Anlegeplatz*

eggshell *Eierschale*

scaly *schuppig*

specs here: parts

chick a baby bird, esp. a young chicken

dusk nightfall

sewing thread ['səʊɪŋ θred] *Nähgarn*

jigsaw cut into different small pieces like in a puzzle

CNN (*abbr.*) Cable News Network, a US news-based pay-television channel

veteran (*US*) sb. who has been in the armed forces during a war

dashboard *Armaturenbrett*

to peer to look carefully or with difficulty

crayon *Wachsmalstift*

Scotch tape *Klebeband; Tesafilm*

engagement ring *Verlobungsring*

to coat to cover sth.

For two days our quiet visitors' parking area outside the trailer park was filled with cars and news trucks and all their broadcasting equipment. Our baby conjoined twin alligators, born from our jigsaw land, were on the national news.

Only one reporter, a tall and slim black woman with light-green eyes wearing a CNN News baseball cap, was interested in our car house. She tripped on us by accident. As she marched toward the river something made her stop at the open window of our car.

My mother was at her job. She worked as a cleaning lady at the veterans' hospital. I was just home from school and making a peanut butter and jelly sandwich on the dashboard.

The reporter leaned over and poked her head inside the Mercury's window. She looked around.

Do you live in here? she asked, and peered into the backseat.

I nodded.

Is that yours? Did you draw that? she asked, and pointed to a crayon drawing of the solar system that was stuck to the back of the driver's seat with pieces of Scotch tape.

On her finger were a gold wedding band and engagement ring with a large diamond.

My eyes always looked at women's hands to see if they were married. My mother said rings were like a passport or a driver's license for love.

I nodded and placed the bread I was coating with a thick layer of blueberry jelly back on the plate.

No, don't stop making your lunch, she said. I'm going to ask you about the baby alligators, okay? But first I need to ask you some basic questions. How old are you?

I'm nine.

I couldn't stop looking at her gold-love-forever rings.

I was nine then. I remember this perfectly because the alligators appeared the week before my tenth birthday. I also think of my life living in the car as divided into two parts – before my mother met Eli Redmond and afterward. Those words – 'before' and 'afterward' – belonged on a clock.

And you live in this car? the reporter asked. She peered in and placed her head almost completely inside the window.

What's your name?

Pearl.

How long have you lived here?

Since being a baby.

But what about a bathroom? she asked.

We use the park, the trailer park's bathroom. The one next to the playground. Sometimes they cut off the water as it smells bad because of the garbage dump. On those days we go to McDonald's and brush our teeth there.

Why does the water smell so bad?

Everyone here knows it's the dump. The garbage is bad for our water.

That's a very fancy plate you're eating on, the reporter said.

I looked at the white porcelain plate covered with delicate pink flowers and green leaves.

It's Limoges, I said. From France.

The reporter was quiet for a few seconds and then asked, Do you like living in a car?

You can get away fast if there's a disaster. Well, that's what my mother likes to say.

The reporter smiled and walked away. She never asked me about the alligators.

Within three days, all the reporters had left because, on the third morning after the discovery, the alligators were dead.

The reporters got in their cars and trucks and U-turned right out of there. It was fast. It was a twenty-minute funeral march.

They sure got out in a hurry. They never even looked over their shoulders to see if they'd forgotten something, my mother said.

We knew those reporters couldn't take the odors from the dump. Our garbage was messing with their perfume.

After the reporters left, my mother slipped on her sneakers, grabbed her frayed straw hat, and got out of the car.

Let's go look at those alligator babies, she said.

As we walked toward the river she took my hand in hers.

We were almost the same size. If someone had watched us as we moved away they could have thought we were two nine-year-old girls walking together toward a swing.

My mother and I walked through the park and along the trail, lined by cypress trees and saw grass, down to the river. As we walked our bodies broke up a cloud of blue and yellow dragonflies that hovered in our path.

The afternoon sun was large above us in a cloudless sky. This made our shadows long and slender and they cast ahead of us as we moved forward. Our shadows, like two friends, led us toward the river.

What's the best thing about living in a car? I asked.

I can tell you. There's no stove with gas burners. As a child, and then growing up, I was always afraid of the gas being left on. I hate the old cabbage smell coming out of a stove. And there's no real electricity in a car, my mother said. And no electrical sockets. You can bet there's always some person who wants to poke some-

fancy extravagant, beautiful

Limoges [li'mɔʒ] expensive porcelain produced in and around the French city of Limoges

to U-turn to turn right back in the direction one came from

funeral march *Trauermarsch*

to mess with sth. to disturb sth., make sth. useless

frayed *ausgefranst*

saw grass *Schilfgras*

dragonfly *Libelle*

to hover to stay in one place in the air by moving the wings quickly

slender thin and delicate

stove a cooker, used to cook and heat food

to poke sth. to push a finger or other pointed objects quickly into sth.

thing into those holes like a hairpin or a fork. I don't have to think about that.

The soft ground leading from our car to the river was a mess. The grass along the path had been trampled and there were a few plastic water bottles, crushed cans, and white lumps of chewing gum left behind. Under a cypress tree there was a length of coiled black electrical cable.

My mother and I expected to see the dead alligators, but when we reached the riverbank they were gone.

The white sand, where the creatures had been the day before, was red sand. Only a tiny pulp of scale and flesh remained tied to the blue thread.

The bullets had torn the newborns to shreds.

The shooters had left behind a few spent casings and shells on the ground nearby.

We never wondered about it. Some person was forever in the mood for target practice. There was always someone skulking around with an itchy trigger finger. Those babies never had a chance.

One time we even found a bullet hole in our car. It had pierced the hood and must have lodged somewhere in the motor because we couldn't find the bullet or exit hole.

When did this happen? my mother said on the day we discovered the clean hole in the steel with a dark ring of residue around it. We never felt it.

People are hunting cars these days, she said. That's a joke. It must have been a stray.

But we both knew this was not unusual. In our part of Florida things were always being gifted a bullet just for the sake of it.

lump *Klumpen*
coiled *gespult*
pulp a soft, wet mass
scale *Schuppe*
shred a small, thin piece
bullet ['bʊlɪt] a small metal object that is shot from a gun
casing *(Patronen)Hülse*
shell *(US) Patrone*
target practice *Zielschießen*
to skulk around to move around or hide, usually with bad intentions
itchy *juckend*
trigger finger the finger that sb. uses to shoot a gun
to pierce *durchbohren*
hood *Motorhaube*
to lodge to become stuck in one place
residue *Schmauchspuren*
stray *Irrläufer*
to be gifted with sth. to get sth. as a present
just for the sake of it just for fun, without any reason

3

On rainy mornings, with the car windows blurred with water, I never daydreamed about a house. That dream was too big. My dreams were about furniture. I imagined having a chair and a desk.

At night I placed a pillow over the hand brake so that the two front seats became one bed. In the dark space of the brake and accelerator pedals, I kept a pair of tennis shoes and sandals.

My books and comic books were laid out in short piles in a row along the dash board and were warped from the sun shining on them day after day.

We kept our groceries in the trunk and ate foods that didn't need refrigeration.

Our clothing was folded into plastic supermarket bags.

In the glove department we kept our toothbrushes, toothpaste, and soap. In this space my mother also kept the can of Raid Flying Insect Killer. Every night before we went to sleep, we closed the windows and sprayed the inside of the car with the insecticide. Every morning as we stretched and yawned, the taste of Raid filled our mouths and mixed with the breakfast taste of Cheerios and powdered milk mixed with water.

In that car my mother taught me how to set a table and how to serve tea. She showed me how to make a bed using a dishcloth folded around a book.

My mother knew about these things because she was raised in a big house with a veranda and swimming pool and five bathrooms. She had servants and a play room where she kept all her toys. She knew how to play the piano and how to speak French, because a French tutor came to her house twice a week during her childhood. When she was in a good mood, my mother's talk always had French words in it. When she was seven, she was given a Shetland pony for her birthday.

My mother's name was Margot, after Margot Fonteyn, the great ballerina. My mother was delicate and graceful. Her neck was even long and slim like a dancer's. She had thin limbs, long fingers, and yellow hair that was spongy and made a yellow cloud all around her head.

By the time I was eleven, my mother and I were the same size and I never grew any taller.

You're the apple on my apple tree, she said.

My mother named me Pearl because, she said, You were so white. You came from a place that is far away from any normal birthplace like a hospital or clinic.

to blur *verschwimmen*

hand brake *Handbremse*

accelerator *Gaspedal*

to warp *sich verziehen*

groceries the food or other items you buy in a supermarket
trunk *(US) Kofferraum*

glove department *Handschuhfach*
Raid brand name of a bed bug, flea and insect killer

to yawn *gähnen*

Cheerios a popular brand of breakfast cereal

Margot Fonteyn (1919 – 1991) English ballerina and dancer with the Royal Ballet
delicate *zart, zerbrechlich*
graceful *anmutig, graziös*
limb an arm or leg of a person or animal
spongy soft

She said, Nobody knew, and I gave you your birthday, to you all alone, by myself, in silence. I did not cry and you did not cry.

I used the bathroom near my bedroom because it had a long, wall-to-wall bathtub, she said. I had to think about everything I needed to do. I lay down in the bathtub like it was a bed. I placed towels down first and a blanket and then I lay down.

My mother was so small, a bathtub was the perfect size for her.

While I lay there, waiting for you to come to me, she said, I breathed in and out.

From the bathtub she could look out the window, through the palm trees of her family's garden, at the sky.

While waiting for you I prayed the rosary, she said. When you pray the rosary your life stops.

She watched the sunset and sunrise.

And you came to me early with the birds, she said. I heard them outside the window.

After she'd cleaned her body, she washed me in the sink with a bar of Avon soap and patted me dry with Kleenex.

She said, You were so small. You fit inside a hand towel. You were so white. More like a pearl than skin. You were like ice or cloud, like a meringue. I could almost see inside your body. I looked at your pale-blue stone eyes and named you. Just that, she said.

I was a pearl. People stared at me. I didn't know a different life. I didn't know what it was like to walk around and not be noticed. They could think I was beautiful or ugly but, no matter what, everyone stared. Hands were always reaching out to touch my silver hair or the white gaze of my cheek.

You're all luster, my mother said. Being with you is like wearing pretty earrings and a new dress.

My mother lived in her father's house for two months after my birth without anyone knowing I was there.

She said, When I had to go to school or leave to do something, I placed you in the closet in my room, all in the dark, all wrapped up. I made a bed for you on the shoe rack with towels and my sweaters. I nested you there like a kitten. I used paper towels from the kitchen as diapers. The house was so big, no one ever heard you cry.

You were born in a fairy tale, my mother said.

During the time my mother had been pregnant, she'd driven around in search of a place she could park the car and live with me while she looked for a job and a small place to rent. The trailer park was only forty minutes from her father's house.

If you're going to hide, hide close by, my mother said. Nobody thinks you're going to hide in plain sight. There are over one

bathtub *Badewanne*
towel *Handtuch*
rosary *Rosenkranz*
sink *Waschbecken*
Avon a US direct selling company in beauty, personal care and household products
to pat sb. dry *jdn. trocken tupfen*
meringue [məˈræŋ] *Baiser, Schaumgebäck*
gaze here: softness
luster (*US*) brightness
closet a cupboard or small room with a door, used to store things
to wrap sth. up *etw. einwickeln*
shoe rack *Schuhregal*
diaper (*US*) *Babywindel*

hundred thousand people missing in this country. If they can't find those people, how are they going to find us?

My mother picked this spot because it had a public recreational area with a bathroom. She always thought we would be there only for a few months.

We had a place to start our living together, my mother said. I cleaned it. And, over the months while I waited for your birth, I stole everything from my parents' house I thought we might need.

Two months after my birth, two months before her exams, and two days before she was going to be seventeen, she drove away from home and never went back.

I didn't look over my shoulder, she said. Don't ever look over your shoulder, because it can make you want to walk backward. Don't ever twist and turn and look over your shoulder, because you might break in two pieces. If anyone ever looked for me after I ran away, they didn't look hard enough because I was never found.

I never had a birth certificate. My mother falsified one copied from the Internet so that I could enroll at the local public school, but my birth was never registered.

Don't worry about yourself, my mother said. You'll never be found, because you've never been missing.

Every time she talked to me about my birth she said, That green-tiled bathroom with a toilet, bathtub, and sink was my manger.

One night, a few weeks after the appearance and death of the conjoined twin alligators, my mother and I were talking in the dark before going to sleep as we did most nights.

We almost always told each other about our day. I'd tell her about school, which was a forty-five-minute walk down the highway to the town, and my mother would recount her day at the veterans' hospital.

Those men are hurt and angry, but they're full of the national anthem, she said. Pearl, it's important to know the world's geography, because the vets hate it if people don't know the places they've been to fight.

I knew the words 'got some' meant the soldier had killed enemy combatants.

As my mother told me the stories she heard from the soldiers, the wars outside in the world came into our car.

My days at school were never as interesting, although there were often fights or kids being caught with cigarettes or a gun in their school bag. I kept to myself and didn't have any close friends except for April May, who lived in our trailer park.

It didn't take long for my mother to figure out what people thought about us. I'd guessed it on my very first days of school: if

to twist here: to turn around

to falsify sth. *etw. fälschen*

to enroll to put yourself on an official list for an activity; *sich einschreiben*

green-tiled *grün gekachelt*

manger *Krippe*

national anthem a country's official song; *Nationalhymne*

vets abbreviation for veterans

combatant ['kɒmbətənt] (*fml.*) a person who fights in a war

bag lady a woman who has no home and carries everything that she owns around with her in bags
contagious *ansteckend*
cricket *Grille*
to croak *quaken*
to fog up *beschlagen*
to be on the prowl to move around an area and look for sb./sth.; *auf Beutezug sein*
to alight to come down from the air and land
the Great Brilliance a state of perfection and a feeling of peace and safety
rustle *Rascheln*
pant *Keuchen*
squeak *Quietschen*
sigh *Seufzer*
to hunger to want sth. very much

you were living in a car, it meant you were just pretending you were not a bag lady not living under a bridge. People were always thinking homelessness was contagious.

Even with the Mercury's doors closed and the windows rolled up with a tiny space open at the top for air, we could still hear the crickets outside. The croaking sound of frogs coming from the river mixed with the noise from cars and trucks driving up and down the highway.

My mother's hand reached toward me, through the space between the door and seat, and softly rubbed my head.

I looked out of the front window and my mother looked out of the back window.

Do you see any stars? she asked after a while.

No. Can you?

The car windows were beginning to fog up. beschlagen

No. There're no stars tonight, not one, but I do feel them. They're coming now.

What do you feel? Who's coming?

Don't you feel it? Indian ghosts are on the prowl tonight.

I don't hear anything. auf Beutezug sein

My mother stopped rubbing my head.

Feel it, she said. Close your eyes.

No. Nothing.

But don't you feel it? They're coming through the trees, from the dump. She said.

Yes. Maybe. No.

There're two. Yes, two of them. Yes.

Are you sure?

Yes, I'm sure. They alight.

What?

Yes, they alight. They've come to take the spirit of those alligators away with them. Every time things go wrong on their land, they come. It's the Great Brilliance.

How do you know?

Just feel it. rascheln

I closed my eyes but could hear only the rustle of my mother's body in the backseat and hear her breath go out, out, out like a gentle pant. I never once heard her breathe in.

I closed my eyes and listened to the strange soft squeaks or sighs the car sometimes made when the air outside grew dense and cold.

I can see there's no silver bullet to end this life, this one-dollar-bill lifestyle, my mother said. We must remember to buy a lottery ticket tomorrow. It hungers me just to think about it.

Yes, I said.

want something very much

You know, my mother said after a few minutes. Sometimes I'm taken over by a great wish to start all over. I want to fall in love with my future again.
My mother was always full of birthday-candle wishes.

4

Once, after Eli had come into our lives, I found my mother all alone in the backseat of the car. I was coming home from school and she should have been at work.

My mother was wearing a light-blue cotton summer dress and she still had her shoes on, which she never did. We always took off our shoes when we were in the car.

What happened to you? I asked. Why aren't you at work?

Words are only meaningful if they're true, my mother said. I think Eli lies to me. He doesn't talk about his life. If I ask him a question, he changes the subject. I can't see inside.

My mother could see inside a person and see broken glass. She could see splinters inside their bodies and the bottles filled with tears.

I can see broken windows, my mother said. In a person's body I can see the bathtub's dirt ring and cigarette burns in the carpet. I can see all the little white Bayer aspirins.

My mother said these feelings increased with every birthday. I remember my piano lessons, she said.

My mother had studied the piano ever since she was six years old at a private music school, until it closed when she was fifteen. Then she took private piano lessons at her home from Mr. Rodrigo until the moment we drove away.

Mr. Rodrigo was a musician from Cuba who had studied in Vienna and London and could have been a great concert pianist. He also taught my mother to love blues and jazz.

Of course, He never became famous, my mother said. He only became a teacher because he had to support his wife and two children. But I also knew there was another reason. Mr. Rodrigo would clap to keep time, and every clap was a slap and a spank and a whipping. Every clap to the metronome was a night of going to sleep without supper. I could see the childhood bruises and broken bones under his grown-up skin. Every piano lesson, every time, after playing the warm-up scales, the room began to smell of Merthiolate.

Do you miss your piano? I asked.

Yes, and also Mr. Rodrigo. He was that kind of man who knew all anyone really needed was to listen to a song and be swayed.

Since she could see under the rind and husk, my mother was always getting mixed up, stirred up with a spoon, shaken like a milkshake with the wrong people all the time.

Once she let an eighteen-year-old hitchhiker stay in the Mercury with us for two days. I moved into the backseat with my mother and he took my place in the front. He was so thin, the belt loops

to change the subject to start talking about sth. else
splinter *Splitter*
cigarette burn *Brandlöcher*
carpet *Teppich*
to clap *klatschen*
slap a quick hit with the flat part of the hand
spank *Klaps*
whipping *Tracht Prügel*
metronome *Taktmesser*
bruise *Prellung, Bluterguss*
Merthiolate *quecksilberhaltiges Antiseptikum*
to sway to move slowly from side to side; here: be influenced or affected by
rind and husk *Rinde und Schale*
belt loop *Gürtelschlaufe*

on his jeans almost came together with the cinched leather belt that held them on his hips. The belt buckle was silver with a gold eagle in the center.

The veins along the young man's arms stood out like branches.

You can see the tree inside that man, my mother said.

He had pale skin, dark blue eyes, and long eyelashes, and he was as small as we are. He was from California and was kind and well-mannered. He said his parents were schoolteachers.

He was a runaway. When he told his parents he was going to leave they'd laughed and said, If you leave just don't come back. They didn't believe him. They thought he was joking.

My mother called him Mr. Don't Come Back.

I'm a runaway too, my mother said to him. Runaways need to take care of each other. Anyway, she added. I can see you're a boy who never had a dream. You never went to sleep and had a dream. You're only living half a life. You don't have the other side. You have the life side; the death side will come, but no dream side. If there's no dream then there's no vigil of the dream. You're not keeping watch.

My mother was right. The runaway never slept. His eyes were always open.

You're making a mistake, my mother said to him. You need to rest. If I had a sport, if someone asked me what my sport was, I'd have to say sleeping.

It was because of Mr. Don't Come Back that I found out about my mother's father and the reason she'd left her home.

Mr. Don't Come Back had been with us for one day and one night. We were outside the car, leaning against the trunk and looking at the cars and trucks pass on the highway. My mother was peeling an orange and giving Mr. Don't Come Back the full juicy wedges for him to suck on. She's already decided he was shipwrecked and had scurvy since she believed you don't have to be adrift on an ocean to be shipwrecked.

I was chewing a piece of gum and wondering how long my mother was planning to let Mr. Don't Come Back hang around. I was ready for him to move out.

So, Mrs. Lady, he asked, why are you living in this car with your baby girl?

My mother didn't answer.

And look, he said, stepping away from the car and pointing. The grass has grown tall around the tires. This old car hasn't been driven in years. The tires are even flat.

I know. I know, my mother said. I really don't have anywhere to drive to, not really.

So why? Why are you living here?

cinched bound firmly

belt buckle *Gürtelschnalle*

branch *Ast*

vigil [ˈvɪdʒəl] *Mahnwache*

wedge a piece of sth. in the shape of a triangle; *Keil*

scurvy *Skorbut*

to be adrift here: not having a clear purpose in life or knowing what to do

tire (*US*) *Reifen*

fly swatter *Fliegenklatsche*
butterfly *Schmetterling*
to whack at sb. to hit sb. noisily
beetle *Käfer*
ant *Ameise*
to squash to crush sth. into a flat shape; *zerquetschen*
to meet with sth. (*phr. v.*) to cause a particular reaction
disapproval *Missbilligung*
church claps rhythmic clapping to hymn singing
firecracker *Frosch (Knallkörper)*
cutthroat *Halsabschneider*
runt (*infml.*) a small and weak person who you dislike
pew *Kirchenbank*

The answer is easy. My father had a fly swatter in every room of our house, my mother said. That's why I left.

As she said these words, I became still and held my breath. My chewing gum came to a full stop in my mouth.

The fly swatters would be hanging from a hook or lying under a windowsill. My father had many and was always swatting something until it was dead, my mother explained. He even used it on butterflies. So he liked to take a whack at me. And he always looked to step on things like a beetle or an ant. My father had shoes on his feet to crush and squash and kick. You can't go around killing little things. And he never went to work. He never had a job. I did leave him a note to say I'd left because he wasn't going to come or go looking. My father thought I'd be back when I ran out of money. He must still be waiting.

You never asked him for money, Mrs. Lady? the runaway asked, but then corrected himself. Of course you never asked him for money. You don't even need to answer my stupid question. People think that runaways have no pride but we're full of pride like a pride bank.

Pearl, my mother said to me. I saved you from a fly swatter. As a kid, I always wondered one thing. It was a question inside me all the time. Do people in other houses wash their fly swatters?

It's good you left your daddy, Mrs. Lady, the runaway said. You can't have some old man swatting your baby girl. That's just the worst thing I ever heard.

These words made my mother fill up with joy as if he were giving her a Being a Good Mother diploma. Usually everything my mother did was met with disapproval, as if not having a front door to open made you unworthy of a job or friendship or someone lending you something. People were always shaking their heads at our life.

My mother never forgot about Mr. Don't Come Back. She said his hands were full of church claps. They understood each other. His one-sided life made her anxious and she'd bring him up from time to time.

Of course, he was a firecracker you could burn your fingers on, she said. Of course, he was a cutthroat and a runt. If you don't dream at night then only this life matters. There's nowhere else to go. I sure don't miss his bag-of-broken-bones body.

Since my mother translated the world for me, I understood everyone was walking around with secrets and broken bones and hurtful words that could not be washed away with soap.

At church she'd scan the pews, bend toward me, and whisper, Pearl, sweetheart, all the people in here are afraid they're going to die.

to dislike somebody who you feel has treated you badly

Since she felt the fragility of everything, it was impossible for her to hold a grudge against anyone. She was sugar. And she always had a box of Domino sugar cubes instead of candy. When I kissed her cheek I could taste the grains. If I were sad about something, she'd give me a cube to suck on.

So, the truth of it all is this: my mother always said that the day she met a murderer, she'd be feeling that the man's shoes were too tight.

And she could see into me too. Once she said, Baby Pearl, don't love me so much. I'm not worth it.

fragility *Zerbrechlichkeit*

to hold a grudge against sb. to have a feeling of anger and dislike for sb. who you feel has treated you badly

grain *Körnchen*

5

The Mercury was full of things my mother had stolen from her house when she ran away.

I thought about this carefully during the nine months before you were born, she said. I knew I had to take the kind of things I'd never be able to buy. I wanted you to see the life you came from. This car is not your only heritage.

I liked to stand outside when she placed the key in the Mercury's lock and turned. The trunk would open, lift slowly, and I would look inside and see gold and silver beneath the groceries. There was the shimmer of beautiful boxes made of cardboard lined with white paper, wood and leather boxes with fine gold latches.

One long, green felt bag with a red silk drawstring contained a Chinese hand-carved ivory boat. It had been made with masts and sails carved from one elephant tusk, which was as long as my arm. There were also small figures of sailors in the boat who were holding on to oars or leaning against one of the masts. This had belonged to my mother's great-grandfather.

Wrapped in tissue was an antique music box made of mahogany and inlaid with shells. It had a piece of glass on one side so that you could watch the lever move and the pins pluck the comb teeth while it played 'The Blue Danube.'

There was a black leather violin case, which contained my great-grandfather's violin.

My mother said, Obviously it is not a Stradivarius, but it is a very fine Italian violin.

At the very back of the trunk there was a long, flat box lined on the outside in light yellow raw silk and wrapped with a dark yellow silk ribbon. We never opened that box because it contained my grandmother's silk chiffon wedding dress, and my mother didn't want it to get dirty.

My mother had two plates of Royal Limoges porcelain, two Baccarat Massena crystal wineglasses, and a five-piece sterling flatware set for two.

She taught me how to hold china up to the light and know if it was porcelain. I needed to see if it was translucent, almost transparent.

I learned about the difference between glass and crystal and the importance of the sound they made. I came to appreciate the craft in making the stem, lip, and bowl of a wineglass.

Once in a while she'd lift everything out of the trunk and bring out the silk bag of jewels. She had a diamond ring surrounded by rubies that had belonged to her French great-grandmother. The bag also contained a rope of pearls and was the longest length

heritage *Erbe*
latch *Riegel, Verschluss*
felt *Filz*
drawstring *Zugschnur*
hand-carved *handgeschnitzt*
ivory *Elfenbein*
tusk *Stoßzahn*
oar *Ruder*
inlaid *mit Einlegearbeit*
lever *Hebel*
to pluck sth. to pull sth.
comb teeth *Kammzähne*
The Blue Danube *An der schönen blauen Donau;* a waltz by Austrian composer Johann Strauss II, composed in 1866
Stradivarius a very expensive type of violin made by the Stradivarius family in the 17th and 18th centuries
Baccarat Massena crystal glass crystal glassware made by the French manufacturer Baccarat (founded in 1764)
flatware set silverware for eating and serving food; *Besteck*
translucent *durchscheinend*
craft *Kunstfertigkeit*
stem *Stiel*
ruby *Rubin*

one could buy. She taught me that ropes of pearls were measured in inches. The sizes were described as collar, choker, princess, matinee, opera, and rope.

In the backseat I also learned how to tell if a pearl was real or made of plastic by softly grinding it between my teeth.

Along with these treasures was my mother's own tiny pink plastic baby bracelet from the hospital tagged with her name on it. Scrawled in black ink, it read her surname and sex: *France. Girl.*

These jewels were never worn. The only thing she wore every day was a small silver ring with a tiny round, blue opal given to her by Mr. Rodrigo, the piano teacher. He'd given it to her because there was a superstition in Cuba that if you wore an opal, the stone had an effect on the piano and bewitched the instrument. She always missed the piano.

My mother liked to kneel on the passenger's side and lean forward and play the piano along the dashboard. From middle C, which was under the rearview mirror, her hands moved in and out along the gray and dirty plastic. Her fingers went back and forth, her thumbs dipped under her palms to reach the keys and hit both sharps and flats. Every now and again, one hand crossed over the other and then rose in the air, suspended for a second, before falling back down to begin the up-and-down race again.

That was Mozart, she said. Did you like it?

Or she said, Those were finger exercises.

I couldn't tell the difference. She heard hammers beating on strings but I only heard the tap-tap-tap of her fingers on the dashboard.

We liked to go on pretend road trips. I played that we were really driving somewhere. My mother always went along with my game.

I was the driver. The seat would be pushed forward but my legs were still too short to reach the pedals. I steered the wheel, turning it in my hands, and pretended to drive.

My mother would sit next to me on the passenger side. She'd check her lipstick in the rearview mirror, put on her sunglasses, and turn on the radio. My mother always made sure the car battery worked and, over the years, we bought new ones. This was the only maintenance she did on the car.

We'd put on our seat belts.

Okay, let's go on a road trip, my mother would say. Leave skid marks. Go over the speed limit. Drive fast. Let's get a ticket.

Where do you want to go? I'd ask.

On our pretended drives my mother talked about her life.

I'd pretend to turn the wheel and she'd talk about St Augustine, where she grew up.

inch 1 inch = 2.54 cm
collar *Halsband*
choker a necklace 34 cm long
princess a necklace 43 cm long
matinee a necklace 60 cm long
opera a necklace 66 cm long
rope a necklace at least 91 cm long
to grind sth. to rub sth. against a surface
to tag sth. *etw. mit einem Anhänger versehen*
to scrawl to write sth. quickly
to bewitch sth. *etw. verhexen*
rearview mirror *Rückspiegel*
palm *Handfläche*
key *Taste*
sharp *Kreuztonart*
flat *Halbton (mit b-Vorzeichen)*
to suspend to stop temporarily
hammer part of the piano that hits the strings to make a sound
string *Saite*
maintenance the work needed to keep a machine in good condition
skid mark *Bremsstreifen*
ticket *Strafzettel*

I knew from my classes in history at school that St Augustine was founded by the Spanish in 1565 and that the area had been populated by the Timucua Indians.

mansion *Herrenhaus*
hanger *Kleiderbügel*
to line sth. *etw. überziehen*

Our house was a large mansion surrounded by oak trees, my mother said. I had two closets for my clothes and all the hangers were lined with pink satin.

palm *Handfläche*

When she spoke she'd often reach out and gently rub my cheek with the back of her hand. It was as if a touch with the back of her hand were more gentle and loving than to touch me with her open palm.

I'd keep my eyes on our imaginary road.

I can't believe we're still living in this car, she said. I always thought we'd only live here for a few months while I get a job and could rent a small house. I'm so sorry, Pearl.

She was an only child in a house filled with servants.

to squat *hocken*
Troy city in ancient Greece; *Troja*

Squatting on the seat beside me, my mother sometimes placed her feet on the dashboard and leaned over and painted her toenails and fingernails a bright red. The color was called Meet Me on the Star Ferry. She picked her nail polish by the name on the bottom of the bottle. She had nail polish called Melon of Troy, Surfing for Boys and Twenty Candles on My Cake.

merry-go-round *Karussell*
protective plastic *Plastikschutzunterlage*

For my tenth birthday my father rented a merry-go-round and set it up on the front lawn of my house, my mother said. It ruined the grass forever after. The men who set it up just trampled all over the lawn, hammered holes into it, and allowed the motor oil from the merry-go-round to spill everywhere. Why did they ruin the grass? Why? They could have put cardboard down or some kind of protective plastic, she said. That grass was suffering.

How did you know?

Pearl, you could just feel it. One day a scientist is going to hear everything the plants are saying. Just wait for the day when trees can tell us what it's like to have their branches cut back. That day is coming soon. Then the world is going to have a real shock.

weary ['wɪəri] very tired
to hold on tight *sich festklammern an*

On these pretend road trips, even though my arms became weary from holding on to the steering wheel, I held on tight so my mother wouldn't stop talking.

to spill *verschütten*
pool *Lache*
puddles *Pfütze*

Your grandmother died in a car crash, she said. A Pepsi truck crashed right into her. The broken Pepsi bottles spilled everywhere. There were pools and puddles of it. My white socks were brown and sticky and my shoes stuck to the pavement.

Where were you going?

pediatrician [piːdiə'trɪʃən] a doctor who has special training in medical care for children

We were going to the pediatrician. I was in the backseat. I was five. I was sick, I had a fever.

And what happened?

You know, I was only just a little piece of a person. I don't remember everything.

It didn't matter how many times my mother told me those events. I wanted to hear about my grandmother's death again and again. I was open-armed for any tragic story.

Before the ambulance arrived, my mother said, I could hear what she was thinking as she died. I could hear the sound of our crushed car. I guess it was the motor making noises. It was creaking and there was some air streaming out of something. But then there was a quiet before the police cars and the ambulance arrived.

How long were you trapped in the car?

I don't know exactly, but it took them at least an hour to untangle the car from the truck and get us out.

What did she say? What did your mother say?

I always asked even though I knew the answer.

She didn't say this aloud. Of course she didn't say this aloud, but I heard it. No one believed me. I was only five and no one ever believes a five-year-old.

I believe you, I said.

My mother lifted her hands and blew over the wet red polish on her fingernails.

I don't think she spoke the words, my mother said, but I heard them: Is this in the Lamb's Book of Life?

She said that? Just that?

Yes. That's what she said. *Is this in the Lamb's Book of Life?* Those were the only words.

In the visitors' parking area of the trailer park there was no movement forward. There was no voyage. Our car faced the same wall and trees.

Do you remember her?

Yes.

I looked over at my mother's ballerina face. She was looking out the window toward the highway.

My mother said, I know that memory is the only substitute for love.

When Eli came into our lives, my mother stopped playing her pretend piano and the stories about her own childhood stopped. Now she was telling Eli those stories. I knew it because he once bought her a bottle of Pepsi. She said it was just his idea of a joke but she also said it wasn't funny.

open-armed welcoming

to untangle sth. here: to separate sth.

the Lamb's Book of Life reference to the New Testament; *die Offenbarung des Johannes; die Apokalypse*

voyage journey

substitute *Ersatz*

6

My best and only friend, April May, lived in a large silver trailer at the back of the park, close to the dump. Even though she was two years older, we were in the same class and she was my only real friend.

The small public school we went to was always threatening to lose its federal funding and shut down because there were so few families in the area with children. Over the past three decades, most people had moved away from small towns and to the cities, where it was easier to find work. Many rural schools had already been closed and we knew it was only a matter of time.

At my school there were only six students in my class and we had the same teacher for every subject. My mother didn't let me spend time with anyone but April May. She didn't want strangers asking me questions. Her constant fear was that I'd be taken from her and placed into foster care.

There's always someone out there who wants to do you a favor, my mother said.

The truth is, no one was knocking on our car door and wanting to be my friend and share a candy bar.

April May's parents let my mother use their trailer as an address when I needed to register for school, or when documents required an address.

I almost always did April May's homework. She had no head for it, but she was not stupid. I didn't mind because it was so easy for me, as my mother had taught me so many things way before they'd ever come up in school.

April May had red hair and was covered with so many freckles that her skin looked reddish brown. My mother called us Ice and Fire.

April May was bossy and I liked this about her because my mother wasn't. My mother never told me to do anything except to make sure I had some dreams when I went to sleep.

My mother said she and I belonged to the Dream Tribe.

It doesn't take too long to figure out that dreams are better than life, my mother said.

April May was so bossy, I called her the cover-your-mouth-when-you-cough police, the don't-talk-back-at-me police, and the eat-with-your-mouth-closed police. She was bossy because her father had been in the army and treated her like a soldier.

I didn't mind her bossiness because she loved to dare me to do things and there were few things I liked more than a dare.

If April May said let's go walk along the river, I said yes.

federal funding money the US government makes available for each state to pay for projects and research

rural in the countryside

candy bar *Schokoriegel*

to require to need sth.

freckles *Sommersprossen*

bossy (*disapproving*) telling others what to do

tribe *(Volks-)Stamm*

to dare sb. to do sth. to ask sb. to do sth. that involves risk

dare sth. difficult or dangerous you do because sb. dares you to do, a challenge

If she said let's go to the candy store and you steal some gum, I said yes.
My mother said I was born under the Risk Star. If you're not careful, she said, someday you're going to try to cross the tracks and outrun a train. If we had a roof, you'd be jumping off of it.
If April Amy said let's explore the garbage dump and I dare you to open the thick black plastic bags, I said yes, yes, yes.
We knew one day we'd find a body in one of those bags. The crime scene was living in our imaginations all the time. We'd already found dead frogs and cats.
The garbage dump was the small local community dump behind the trailer park. A row of sand pines shielded the view, but nothing could buffer the smells and the sound of the garbage trucks. The shriek of rusted hinges as a truck's rear loader lifted and dropped the garbage mixed with the sound of wind and rain as if it were part of nature.
We were told not to go near the dump because it was dirty, full of things that were rotten, and, because of this, could make us sick. April May's mother, Rose, even said that there were toxic materials and medical waste from the local veterans' hospital, where she and my mother worked. But we went anyway.
A sign outside the dump wired to the fence said DANGER DO NOT ENTER, but there was no gate or lock or guard.
There was a small tree to one side of the entrance. This tree had been used as target practice and was full of holes. There were many places in the tree where I could see right through the orange-brown bark.
Even with all the rot, the dump was mostly a landscape of plastic in every color and broken pieces of glass shone among the junk like green and blue crystals. There were plastic dishes, spoons, forks, bags, boxes, bottles, and doll parts, Barbie doll heads without bodies and with matted yellow, orange, or red hair lay among broken eggshells and milk cartons. There were pairs of pink plastic legs, or a solitary leg poking out of a red box of Lucky Charms, pink arms, and even pink torsos with belly buttons.
Once April May found a pair of old jeans with a ten-dollar bill sticking out of the back pocket. We couldn't believe it. From then on we always looked inside the pockets of any discarded, frayed clothing we found.
On one of these scavenger trips I found a broken thermometer in a small box. The silver mercury was fragmented into balls. As I played with the shiny liquid silver, moving it around on the surface of my palm, the mercury broke into small slippery drops and melded back into one large bead. I rolled the liquid metal off my hands and into the pocket of my jeans.

to shield to hide sth.
to buffer to provide protection against sth.
shriek *Gekreische*
hinge *Drehgelenk*
rear at the back
loader a machine used for putting heavy things on a vehicle
toxic poisonous; *giftig*
bark *Rinde*
junk *Schrott*
matted *verfilzt*
solitary being the only one
to poke out of *herausstechen*
Lucky Charms a US brand of cereal
belly button (*infml.*) *Bauchnabel*
to discard to throw away
frayed *ausgefranst*
scavenger *Plünderer; Lumpensammler*
mercury *Quecksilber*
to meld *schmelzen*
bead *Perle*

marble *Murmel*
hoop ring-shaped
brass *Messing*

When I got back to the car, I placed the mercury in a small bag, which I kept under the front seat of the car. The bag contained all the things I'd kept from the dump. I had some marbles, one gold hoop earring, and four brass buttons made with the image of a ship's anchor on each side.

moth *Motte*
species ['spi:ʃi:z] *Gattung*

One time April May found a cardboard box full of large black and brown moths. At first glance one of the insects was so large, I thought it was a bird. The moths were laid out one on top of the other, with slim pieces of white tissue paper between each moth. Inside the box there was also a piece of paper with the names of the species written in ink. The list read: Atlas Moth, Black Witch, Comet Moth, Luna Moth, Death-Head's Hawkmoth, and Heart and Club Moth.

to dissolve to disappear; *sich auflösen, zerfallen*
spell spoken words that are thought to have magical power; *Zauber(-spruch)*
superstitious/superstition *abergläubisch/Aberglaube*

We tried to pick them up but, after a few careful attempts, we gave up. The moths dissolved into powder as soon as we touched them.

This is someone's collection, April May said. I'll take it. I can't just leave all these dead moths out here. It's a spell on us. If I leave the moths here, bad things will happen.

April May was so superstitious she even invented her own superstitions on the spot.

Just leave them, I said. They're falling to pieces.

Okay, April May said. But if bad stuff happens, it's our fault.

We were also used to finding stacks and stacks of magazines, especially old *Time* magazines and pornography magazines. We had our sex education out in the dump and saw things no person should ever even hear a rumor about.

There were also baby shoes littered all over the place and some were still in pairs, tied together by their laces.

My mother said, I'm always thinking that the air from that dump blows out into the ocean. Everything in the whole United Sates eventually blows across the country and over the Atlantic. Everything that happens in New York ends up blowing over to Iceland or Ireland. Look up at the sky and you can imagine what it holds. Think of all the party balloons that have floated over to France. Think of all the smoke from the Fourth of July fireworks that has blown out across land and sea to England.

Afghanistan US war in Afghanistan started in 2001 in order to dismantle Al Qaeda and remove the Taliban from power
to caress [kə'res] **sth.** to touch sth. in a gentle and loving way
to tug sth. to pull sth. quickly

April May's father, whom everyone called Sergeant Bob, was a war veteran and had been to Afghanistan. He was one of the very first soldiers to go over, as well as one of the first to come back. Sergeant Bob was a tall man who shaved his head. He had a short beard that grew only on his chin and he caressed it all the time between his fingers or tugged it as if trying to pull it off. He was also missing an ear from the same land mine that blew off his leg.

Sergeant Bob liked to say, with outrage, that he had stepped on a goddamned Russian land mine, as if that made the land mine even more terrible.

outrage a feeling of anger and shock

The explosion had also left him almost completely deaf, and so we had to scream when we wanted to speak to him.

Sergeant Bob said that now that he had only one leg and couldn't hear anything, he'd discovered books. He could order books through the VA Lending Library catalogs, which operated all over the country.

Sometimes he wore his prosthetic leg, but mostly he limped around on crutches and with the empty pant leg pinned up with a large diaper safety pin. Sergeant Bob rarely wore a shirt, and he had tattoos all over his upper body. He was inked after two of his friends died in Afghanistan.

prosthetic [prɒsˈθetɪk] artificial
to limp *humpeln*
crutch *Krücke*
safety pin *Sicherheitsnadel*
to ink sb. (*infml.*) to tattoo sb.

Sergeant Bob said, The most painful place to be tattooed is on the skin over the ribs.

On his left side and above his waist was written: *In memory of fallen coMr.ades.* On the right side the tattoo said: *In God We Trust.*

In God We Trust the official motto of the USA

I was raised Christian, Sergeant Bob said. But I didn't really believe in God until I went to Afghanistan. Those boys who died over there could have been anyone. Every day of my life I look at my tattoos in the mirror and know how lucky I am. I believe in God now because what else are you going to do at my age?

Sergeant Bob had seven cartridges inked on his back with the names of the seven friends he'd lost written on the inside of each of the bullets. Every time I was near Sergeant Bob I couldn't help reading the names: Sean, Mitt, Carlos, Luke, Peter, Manny, and Jose.

cartridge *Patronenhülse*

April May's mother, Rose, was a nurses' assistant at the small veterans' hospital in town. Sergeant Bob met Rose at the hospital. She'd been one of his nurses.

Everyone in the park went to look for Rose if they needed a Band-Aid or an allergy pill. She had it all. Rose also was good at giving someone an injection, cleaning a wound, or putting on a bandage. It turned out that everyone at some point always ended up needing her.

Band-Aid brand name for a small sticky piece of cloth or plastic used to cover a wound; *Pflaster*
bandage [ˈbændɪdʒ] *Verband*

One day April May and I were sitting on the grass outside their trailer with Rose. It was one of those rare days in July when a breeze blew the humidity away and allowed us to sit outside the trailer. Even the smells from the dump were being carried off, away from us, all the way to Sweden.

humidity *Luftfeuchtigkeit*

On these clear days my mother said, Today the waters of Scandinavia are being settled by the particles of waste made up of pollen from Kansas, coal dust from Pennsylvania, and spiderwebs from Vermont.

thigh the part of a person's leg above the knee
Doritos an American brand of flavoured tortilla chips
triangular *dreieckig*
residue sth. that is left after the main part is no longer present; *Rückstand*
Hello Kitty a Japanese fictional cartoon character; a combination of cat and human
true-blue (*old-fashoined*) completely loyal to a person or belief
checkbook *Scheckheft*
cordial (*fml.*) friendly, but formal and polite
ammonia *Ammoniak*
meth lab (*infml.*) an illegal laboratory that produces the drug metamphetamine (crystal meth)
addict *Drogenabhängige(r)*
one-pot meth operation (*infml.*) illegal production of crystal meth in one- or two-litre bottles, making the production easier and cheaper
vent *Entlüftungsöffnung*
spacey (*sl.*) not aware of what is happening around you
cop (*infml.*) police officer
skinny very thin
to grind (ground, ground) one's teeth *mit den Zähnen knirschen*
meth oil colourless oil insoluble in water

Rose was sitting on a lawn chair with a large pink plastic glass between her thighs. The glass was filled with lemonade. She was eating Doritos and licking the salty orange chili and cheddar cheese powder off her fingers after each chip went into her mouth. April May and I were sitting close enough to Rose to hear the first crunch as it broke the triangular chip against her front teeth. She didn't offer us any. When she finished, she wet her pointer finger in the mouth and wiped it along the bottom of the Dorito's bag to pick up the last residue of the powder and then sucked it off. The tip of that finger was always bright red.

Beside her, on the ground, was a can of Pepsi.

Rose had a Hello Kitty tattoo on her right ankle. To show me that her mother was a true-blue Hello Kitty fan, April May once let me take a peek at her mother's Bank of America checkbooks with Hello Kitty printed on them as well as her Visa card, which had a picture of Hello Kitty printed on the plastic.

My mother was extra kind to Rose. They were not really friends but they worked together at the hospital and had a distant, cordial respect for each other.

She's not a foggy day. She's not a cloudy day. But Rose does smell like ammonia, my mother said. It's as if she walked through a cloud of something.

Why?

As a teenager Rose's parents rented a house that had once been a meth lab.

Rose told me about it once, my mother said. Living in that house, Rose started to get sick all the time and feel bad, really bad, and so did her parents. They figured it out when addicts would stop by looking for drugs. That house had been a one-pot meth operation. There had been an explosion in the cooking of the meth and there was residue everywhere, even in the air-condition vents. Rose is spacey. She's sick. Those crystals got into her.

Everyone in Florida knew what a meth lab was. The cops were finding them all the time. It was always on the news and everyone had a story about someone making meth. Everyone in Florida also knew that Mexican heroin was taking over the meth business.

At school we knew one boy, Rusty, who was tall and skinny and always grinding his teeth. He had been put in foster care when his parents went to jail for the production and distribution of meth. It had been bad luck because someone had reported a fire in the woods behind their house, but when the firemen arrived they found an active one-pot lab and 172 grams of meth oil.

Rusty came to school to say goodbye, I told my mother. He told us he was going to foster care somewhere outside Miami. He made me feel so sad. I think everyone at school felt sad.

Yes, of course, my mother said. You were upset because, before you even forgot him, even before he closed the door and walked away, you knew you would forget him.

The job at the veterans' hospital made my mother think about how quickly people are forgotten. She wondered if the worst fate was to be forgotten or to die. There were too many veterans who never had a family member or friend come around to visit.

As Rose ate her Doritos, she spoke to us about love. Rose was worried because April May had no interest in boys or being feminine. April May didn't like Hello Kitty and hated the color pink. She cut her hair short with the kitchen scissors.

That morning, as Rose sucked on her bright-orange Dorito finger and drank the Pepsi, she decided to give us some love instruction. Instead of talking to men, just touch them, she said. No talking. I never thought a man like Sergeant Bob would love me. Keep your eyes open, girls, for a man who really gets it, who knows a woman is paradise. He should deserve your kiss and fuss. Don't talk too much. No blah, blah, blah nonsense. If you want to say something, make the word a rub, make the word a pinch. Every time you're going to talk just touch him instead. Don't say good morning, just touch his shoulder. Don't ever ask him if he loves you; suck his fingers instead. You have to make him some memories. Right? Am I right? You tell me.

And the truth is, Rose did exactly as she said. She never spoke to Sergeant Bob. Instead, we watched as she caressed the top of his head or kissed the back of his neck. Sometimes she'd run her finger over his tattoos as if she were painting them again or following a road map along his body. Under her touch, Sergeant Bob would close his eyes or reach for his wallet and give her a ten- or twenty-dollar bill.

It's true, Meat Mud really loves her. April May said to me one day when we were hanging out down at the river. Even if they are my parents and all, it's kind of disgusting.

April May had nicknames for everyone. Her father was Meat Mud and her mother was Shortnin' Bread.

One Valentine's Day, Sergeant Bob gave Rose a 9mm pistol.

When a man gives his woman a gun it's because he really trusts her, Sergeant Bob said. It won't ever be a widow maker. Some guns are widow makers, but this gun is true blue. It's a lot more useful than a box of candy. I'd rather come home and find the coroner carrying out anyone that was messing with her than find

to get sth. *(infml.)* to understand sth.
fuss attention
rub here: touching sb. in a sexual way
pinch *Kneifen, Zwicken*

Meat Mud name of a US barbecue sauce

Shortnin' Bread name of a classic sweet Southern US dessert

coroner *Rechtsmediziner*
to mess with sb. to attack sb. or use violence against sb.

orphan a child whose parents are dead

to settle a score to punish sb. for sth. wrong they did to you in the past that you cannot forgive; *eine Rechnung begleichen*

holster *Pistolenhalfter*

Walther PPQ.40 semi-automatic pistol developed in 2011 by the German company Walther in Ulm

99.6 degrees Fahrenheit measurement of temperature (= 37.5°Celsius)

to gift sb. sth. to give sb. sth. in an official and formal way

to be born with a silver spoon in one's mouth to be born into a wealthy family

to boast *(lautstark) prahlen, angeben*

fancy decorative

to brag about sth. (*infml.*) mit etw. *prahlen/angeben*

to rumble around *(herum-) poltern*

she'd baked me an apple pie. Yes, that's the truth of it. If a man gives his woman a gun it's because he really trusts her.

Sergeant Bob had all kinds of names for guns. Some were widow maker, orphan maker, and peacemaker. If they were used to steal a car, he called them carmakers and, if a gun missed its mark, he called it a rainmaker. If it settled a score, the gun was a lawmaker. The pistol was pink. He also gave Rose a special pink holster so that she would carry it under her arm, but she was too fat. She just placed the pistol down the front of her blouse between her breasts if she was just hanging around the trailer park or, if she went out, she carried it in her bag.

Rose said, It's the best present ever because he wants me to be safe.

Sergeant Bob didn't want her to have a pink gun because he said no one was going to take that color very seriously if she got into some trouble, but Rose won every argument by just caressing his hair or squeezing the earlobe of his one ear.

I believed in guns before I met my husband, Rose said, so he can't boss me around about guns. My family always had guns growing up. My father hunted. Guns give me freedom. I know this. Anyway, the next pistol on my wish list is a Walther PPQ.40 caliber, and that should make him happy.

My mother thought Rose should not keep the gun down her blouse.

It's like placing a candle near a curtain or drying clothes on a stove, she said. Eventually something is going to burn up.

Rose said, Once you get a gun, you're at 99.6 degrees Fahrenheit all the time. I must say, though, I must admit it, I thought he was going to give me a ring.

My mother said that Rose was a good woman.

She's never met a stranger, my mother said. She's a good nurse. Even when someone's going to die, she tells them they're going to live. She's not gifting anyone some bad news.

When Rose talked about my mother she said, Your darling mama was given a forty-eight deck of cards. God was not counting right for her or somebody stole those four missing cards right up their sleeve. Even though that mother of yours was born with a silver spoon in her mouth, she's a good woman. Your mama is the living proof that a rich person can be a good person. She doesn't boast about her fancy little girl shoes she had and she doesn't brag about fancy words.

Everyone liked my mother. I'm sure this was because she could look into them and see what hurt. What was outside came inside of her and settled in her body as if she were a box or bag for everyone to rumble around inside.

Rose also said, The problem with your mother is she feels everyone's pain and that's not good if you work at a hospital. She has true empathy malady. It's a sickness.

My mother was a cleaning lady at the same veterans' hospital where Rose worked as nurse. It was one of the very few places a person could find a job in our area of Florida. My mother, who did not have even a high school diploma, could only work in the hospital's sanitation department.

My ballerina mother mopped floors, made beds, washed bedpans, emptied garbage bags, and swept hallways. She wore a coat over her clothes, rubber gloves, plastic bags over her shoes, and a hair net that covered her whole head and matted down her blond hair. Both my mother and April May's mother complained about the fact that the vets were not properly treated and that doctors came sporadically and the vets were often made to wait months for treatment. Even the hospital's sanitation department was always running short on everything – even basic supplies like toilet paper and cleaning liquids.

The hospital is a place between heaven and earth, my mother said. How can I explain the place? It's a place where a man can cry like a baby for the loss of his arm. It's where men are paper dolls to be torn up. They know they cannot protect anyone and what's the point in being a man if you can't protect someone?

Rose said the hardest thing about her job were the suicides. Those vets make it through the war and then they go and bump into a razor or a rope, she said.

Once a year, during National Nurse Week, the local church pastor who also lived in the trailer park, Pastor Rex Wood, would go to the hospital for a ceremony he invented called the Blessing of Hands. He liked to think up new religious ceremonies. He called himself a religious innovator.

On Blessing of Hands Day, the nurses would leave their patients and duties for twenty minutes and go outside to the hospital's parking lot. The nurses would line up and hold out their opened palms for the blessing. Pastor Rex would walk up to each of them and sprinkle a little holy water on their hands while he said a prayer.

There were always one or two meth or heroin addicts hanging out in the parking lot who watched the blessing. Most people could tell the difference, because the meth addicts had sores on their faces and meth smiles, which were smiles without teeth or with teeth that had no business being in someone's mouth. The heroin addicts hung around the hospital hoping some nurse might slip them a syringe or a box of laxatives. The heroin users

empathy *Mitgefühl, Einfühlungsvermögen*
malady (*fml.*) a disease

sanitation department *sanitäre Einrichtungen; Reinigungs-*

sporadically sometimes, irregularly

paper doll sth. that has no substance
to tear (tore, torn) up (*phr. v.*) to be pulled to pieces
suicide the act of killing yourself
to bump into sth. (*phr. v.*) to come across or strike against sth.
razor *Rasierklinge, Rasiermesser*

blessing *Segnung*

sore an infected area on the surface of the body; *Geschwür*

syringe [sɪˈrɪndʒ] *Spritze*
laxative *Abführmittel*

were always falling asleep against a car or even under a car in search of shade on a hot sunny day.

Everyone knew that it was the only day of the year when every nurse in that place had her nails done at the local beauty salon. I knew that as my mother watched the blessing, her own hands were wrapped tightly around a mop. The other cleaning ladies kept their hands in their pockets. The cleaning staff never had their hands blessed because nobody ever thought their hands deserved it.

pulpit *Kanzel*

to toil to work hard, esp. physically

Pastor Rex liked to print out his sermons and blessings and hand them out at church. On the Sunday following National Nurse Week he gave out one that he also read aloud from the pulpit. Lord bless the hands that care and toil. Bless the hands that help another walk. Help the hands that inject and hold glasses of water. Help the hands that clean bodies. Help the hands that are more than hands and carry the suffering of the world. Amen.

liar sb. who does not tell the truth; *Lügner*

My mother said, You never know where the devil is hiding. Liars are always pretending to be priests or poets. Liars hide out in the purest places.

After school April May and I liked to go for a walk down to the river, where there was a dock we could sit on and look at the water.

Let's talk about this and that, April May liked to say as we sat down.

to flick across *umherschwirren*

We watched dragonflies flick across the surface and always kept our eyes open for any stirring in the water, which might be the slow movement of an alligator. In Florida everyone knew never to sit on the edge of a dock with your feet in the water. But April May liked to dare me to do it and I always did. When I dared her back, she always refused. We both knew I was the bravest.

Sometimes April May would complain about her mother and father and say, Shortnin' Bread is driving me crazy and Meat Mud is also driving me crazy. They both drive me crazy. How did I get those parents? How?

to shrug to raise and lower your shoulders in order to say that you do not know or are not interested

I always just shrugged at this.

Hey, hey. Well, what about you? Doesn't Margot drive you crazy?

I had to answer no.

No?

No.

to affect sb. to have a negative influence on sb.

Hey, April May said. I heard your mother was always given a little gas from the stove to breathe. I'm sure it had to affect her. It's probably why she's so dreamy.

What do you mean? I asked.

Yes. I heard about it. As a little girl your mother was given gas from the oven to breathe in so she'd go to sleep. Her daddy would hold her over the burner and turn the control knob.

knob *Drehknopf*

Of course I knew about it. My mother told me. Her father said, If a girl doesn't want to go to sleep, a little gas was always better than a glass of milk.

She's just got to make you a little crazy sometimes, April May continued. Come on. Come on. Just admit it. All parents drive their children crazy.

No, I said. Never.

My mother always knew exactly what to say to give me some sweetness and make me smile.

One day my mother said, Pearl, do you know what the best question in the world is? The very best question of all?

No, tell me.

Her old life and new life were always in a mixing bowl like flour and sugar.

Are you going to the ball?

7

The river was also the place where April May and I went to smoke cigarettes, which we had been doing since I was ten and she was twelve.

I was an expert at stealing cigarettes. This, in addition to doing her homework, was my job in the friendship with April May. Everything else was her job. She decided what we were going to do and even directed what we would wear, which meant any color but pink. Any piece of clothing that had a Hello Kitty or a Disney Cartoon character on it was forbidden. She detested the Disney princesses.

to detest sb. to hate sb. very much

Since my job was to find cigarettes, I had to sneak around the park in search of people who smoked. There were not that many people to choose from, as only four trailers on the land were occupied.

Luckily everybody smoked, except for April May's parents and my mother.

I was always sneaking, looking to slip out a few cigarettes from packs that were lying around. If I felt very brave, sometimes I stole whole packs. Often I had to settle with snatching a half-smoked cigarette out of an ashtray. Even on my walks home from school, I'd rescued cigarettes that were lying on the ground and had been stepped on or thrown out a car window.

to sneak to go somewhere secretly
to slip sth. out to remove sth. quickly and easily

One of the homes in the trailer park where I could always find cigarettes belonged to Mrs. Roberta Young. Everyone called her by her whole name. She lived in her trailer with her thirty-year-old daughter, Noelle, two tiny Chihuahuas, and a parrot in a cage. The parrot was kept inside the trailer at night. During the day the cage was placed outside on a plastic chair under the shade of a short palm tree.

Chihuahua [tʃɪˈwɑːwə] a very small dog with large eyes and ears and smooth hair

Noelle never went to school, but she was an electrical genius. Everyone knew that if you had a lamp that didn't work or an electrical socket that sent out a spark, the person to call on was Noelle.

socket *Steckdose*

It was as if she were born from lightning, her mother said. She can fix anything. She can make dead car batteries come back to life just by wiggling the wires.

to wiggle sth. *an etw. wackeln*

Noelle had a large collection of Barbie dolls. The world she had invented around them was all she cared about. Her community of Barbies took up half of the trailer. The dolls were placed standing, lying down, or sitting in all kinds of poses. They all had names and piles of clothes. Noelle kept count of everything and once told me she had sixty-three Barbie dolls. It was all she ever wanted for her birthday or Christmas.

April May didn't like Noelle and would never hang out with her.

April May would run in the opposite direction.

April May believed Noelle could give her an electrical shock and her nickname for Noelle was Voltage.

Noelle had black hair, which she wore in a braid, and dark brown eyes. She walked with a very straight back as if a board were tied at her waist. She also never moved quickly and always walked on tiptoe. *Zeheuspitze*

voltage *elektrische Spannung*

braid *Zopf*

tiptoe *Zehenspitze*

April May said, Just guess who else walks on tiptoe?

Who?

A Barbie doll, of course!

Noelle often gave me math classes. These were observation classes, really, as I watched her do a problem over and over again until I understood. She could not explain in words what her mind was doing.

It took me some time to realize that Noelle, who loved fortune cookies and kept the fortune papers in a plastic bag, had memorized the words as if they were poems.

fortune cookie biscuit containing a piece of paper with a horoscope or maxim on it; *Glückskeks*

A stranger is a friend you have not spoken to yet, she said.

We can't help everyone, but everyone can help someone, she said.

Next full moon brings an enchanting evening, she said.

Is Noelle very sad? I asked my mother.

Yes, she's the worst kind of sad. She doesn't know she's sad. She's a stray.

stray *Streuner*

My mother called anyone or anything that seemed alone, or ended up in the wrong place, a stray. There were stray people, stray dogs, stray bullets, and stray butterflies.

Whenever I went to Noelle's trailer for math class, Mrs. Roberta Young offered me something to eat. She liked to give me a plate of strawberries and say, Strawberries have two hundred seeds on them and they are the only fruit with seeds that grow on the outside. Or she would say things like, Don't miss looking at the new photographs from the Hubble Telescope. She always said, Global warming is real just like the sky is blue.

Hubble Telescope a space telescope launched in 1990

I knew Mrs. Roberta Young was the smartest person I'd ever met. She'd been to the University of Florida and had studied biology. She was a retired high school science teacher who lived off of a Social Security check. My mother told me she'd lost everything, including her house. Her husband had died after a long illness and medical bills had left her almost destitute. *without anything*

Social Security *staatliche Rentenversicherung*

destitute without money, home, food or possessions

The garbage dump was affecting the area, Mrs. Roberta Young claimed, and we were being slowly contaminated. She wrote up petitions and sent these to the local and state governments. But no one ever came to inspect the dump or check on our water.

contaminated polluted, infected, poisoned

- **skink** small lizard
- **centipede** *Tausendfüßler*

Mrs. Roberta Young once found a dead skink with twelve legs, which made it look like a centipede.

- **to shrivel up** *schrumpfen, ausdörren*
- **mildew** *Schimmel*

She kept that skink in her refrigerator for weeks beside the carton of milk and box of eggs as she tried to think of a way to get it to a scientist or environmentalist. As the days passed by, the creature shrank and shriveled up. Mrs. Roberta Young finally threw the skink out when it became coated with a thin film of green mildew, like a piece of bread.

She once told me that ombrophobia is the fear of rain.

Really? Really? Do you know anyone who has that?

Oh, for sure.

Who?

Noelle.

Noelle?

Yes, of course. I know about this fear because it's her problem. Noelle won't go out in the rain. Not ever.

What happens to her?

- **to electrocute** to kill sb. by causing electricity to flow through their body

Noelle thinks she could get electrocuted.

Of course, she thinks she'll be a hair dryer that falls into a bathtub, my mother said.

- **Blaise Pascal** (1623-1662), French philosopher and mathematician
- **wager** ['weɪdʒər] *Wette, dass man weniger riskiert, wenn man an Gott glaubt, als wenn man ihn leugnet*

Mrs. Roberta Young also told me about Pascal's wager. She said, It's about betting with your life if God exists or not.

It's like a dare? I asked.

No, not exactly, she said.

Mrs. Roberta Young and Noelle both smoked Salem menthols, which were my favorites. Neither the mother nor the daughter ever bothered to step outside to smoke, and so their small trailer always smelled like tobacco mixed with rotten fruit from the parrot's cage and dog food from the bowls laid out on the floor of the narrow trailer's hallway.

- **Where there's smoke there's fire.** (*proverb*) if unpleasant things are said about sb., there is probably a good reason for it
- **nostril** *Nasenloch*
- **to stub out** (*phr. v.*) to stop a cigarette from burning by pressing the burning end against a hard surface

Where there's smoke there's fire, Noelle would say as she blew smoke out of her mouth and nostrils.

If I could steal a Salem out of a pack it made my day. And this was because, after I smoked the mentholated cigarette as far down as possible, I'd stub it out and suck on the filter and it was always like having a mint.

Pastor Rex was also a smoker.

Mrs. Roberta Young, like my mother, didn't like Pastor Rex or churches. She said, We lived near a town that has only a few hundred people living in it, but has five churches. This is what America has come to. Someday there will be more churches than schools.

- **wire-rimmed glasses** *Brille mit Drahtfassung*

Pastor Rex was from Texas. He was a short man in his early forties. His head was shaved and he wore round wire-rimmed glasses.

Pastor Rex seemed to be alone in the world. No family ever came to visit him. He said he'd been married, but had no children.

Because of the abundance of churches in our area, Pastor Rex was very proud of the programs he thought up to bring more parishioners to his church. He was particularly satisfied with a program called Drive-Thru Prayer.

On the last Sunday of every month, Pastor Rex had volunteers hold signs on the highway that led into town inviting people to drive into the church's parking lot for a prayer.

Everyone can just pull in, stay inside their cars or trucks, and pray with no strings attached, Pastor Rex said. The Drive-Thru Prayer makes praying easy. They don't even have to turn off their motors or their radios.

April May smiled at this. Because you live in a car, you and Margot do the Drive-Thru Prayer all day and all night, she said. He's an idiot.

Pastor Rex also invented the U-Turn Prayer program.

The U-Turn Prayer, Pastor Rex explained, means that if you're driving down the highway of life in one bad direction, you can just do a U-turn and drive back to the good life where you came from or should've been.

If you're a drug addict, make a U-turn, he liked to say. If you're a wife beater, make a U-turn. If you've forgotten about Jesus Christ, just make a U-turn.

April May said, He forgot to say we need to turn on the turn signal first or you'll get a ticket. He's a stupid idiot.

Mrs. Roberta Young warned me to keep an eye on Pastor Rex.

She said, You better watch it. I don't like that man. Did you know he's the one who shot those two baby alligators?

Pastor Rex told you he's the one who killed them? I asked.

Oh, yes.

But why?

He's proud of it. He said we didn't need reporters and people hanging around and looking into our lives. But this doesn't matter, she said. I'm telling you to keep your eye on what's going on.

Mrs. Roberta Young didn't want my mother to end up with Pastor Rex. She told me that she respected my mother because she was the only well-mannered, properly raised person around.

Your mother comes from finery, she said. Even if she had you, she still knows the true meaning of the word 'please,' which really means 'if you please.' Your mother knows you will always regret the small thing you didn't say for the rest of your life. She's a person who knows she should be wearing white gloves to church even if she doesn't do it.

abundance *Überfluss*

parishioner *Gemeindemitglied*

with no strings attached with no conditions or limitations

finery splendour, a background where everything is refined

to regret *bedauern*

I knew Mrs. Roberta Young was talking about the fact that my mother had me without a husband, without being married and while she was still in high school, and then had run away from home.

My mother never told me who my father was, and the truth is I never asked. I only knew he was a schoolteacher with a family and would have gone to jail if anyone found out he'd loved-up a student.

to love-up sb. (*sl.*) to love sb. very much; *s. an jdn. heranmachen*

My mother didn't want him around, not even in our thoughts.
She didn't want his name being said in our oxygen.
She didn't want him to open the door, walk into my night-time dreams, take a seat, and start talking.
She didn't want him to stir up our life like a spoon because I knew she loved him. Every time she looked at me she saw him.

to stir sth. up (*phr. v.*) to cause an unpleasant emotion or problem to come to the surface again

After Mrs. Roberta Young told me Pastor Rex was trying to court my mother, I watched him closely and, yes, of course, Mrs. Roberta Young was right. He was always looking at my mother as if she were a mirror to look at himself. I could see he wanted to be loving her up in the movies by next Saturday night.

Every other evening, Pastor Rex came over to the Mercury and knocked on the window on the driver's side of the car. I don't know how many times. I had to tell him that he needed to knock on the window of the backseat.

I'd roll down my window and say, Pastor Rex, this is my room! Knock on the backseat window. If you please.

I'm so sorry, Pearl, he'd say every time. Is your mother here?

I don't know.

Really?

Yes. This car is so big I can't find her in here.

Every few weeks he'd leave her a bouquet of flowers on the windshield of the Mercury. When you live in a car, there's no surface for a vase of flowers. My mother would cut the stems short and arrange the flowers in an empty tin of powdered milk that she filled with water. Then she placed the bouquet outside on the roof as if the roof were a mantelpiece.

stem *(Blumen-)Stängel*

powdered milk *Pulvermilch*

mantelpiece *Kaminsims*

My mother was always kind to Pastor Rex because she was kind to everyone.

She said, God is really boxing with that man. Pastor Rex thinks the church is a U-turn or like wearing a new suit. I can see what he really likes to do is count up the money he collects on Sundays.

My mother's kindness kept him in a state of false hope.

Pastor Rex was a secret smoker. Even though he lived by himself, he'd smoke in his bathroom and blow the smoke out the window. I guess he didn't want to catch himself.

So I had to get into his bathroom in order to steal cigarettes, which he kept on the window ledge. There was often a pair of socks drying in his shower and a short stack of *Reader's Digest* magazines on the floor next to the toilet. On the edge of the sink, he had a toothbrush with the plastic grip in the shape of Jesus on the cross. It was easy to steal cigarettes from Pastor Rex because I always knew when he was at church. I also took advantage of his visits to my mother. He'd tap on her window, she'd roll it down, and I'd race out of the car, across the park, past the old swing set, the public bathroom, and to his trailer.

April May didn't believe me when I told her about the toothbrush. She dared me to steal it and bring it to her. So of course I did because I was begging for danger as if it were a sport.

One afternoon, when I knew that Pastor Rex was busy with his Drive-Thru program, I told April May to meet me down at the river, on the dock. Then I went to his trailer, placed the Jesus-on-the-cross toothbrush down the front pocket of my jeans, and snuck down to the river where April May was waiting for me.

I don't want to touch it, she said when I held it out to her.

I told you it was real.

When I explained that I planned to return the toothbrush back to Pastor Rex's bathroom, April May snatched the toothbrush out of my hand.

Oh, no you're not. You're not taking this back, she said.

But he'll miss it. He'll know someone was there.

You're not going to take back something you've stolen, April May said. That would be really stupid. Imagine not getting caught stealing, but getting caught putting something you've stolen back in its place!

Then she lifted her arm up high in the air and cast the Jesus toothbrush into the river.

After this, every time I looked at the river, I knew there were fish and frogs and alligators in that yellow water. I knew there were skinks with twelve legs and frogs with white eyes. Now I also knew there was a Jesus toothbrush lying on the bottom of the riverbed.

The other people who smoked in the park were the Mexican people, Ray and Corazón, who didn't do any of the things everyone else liked to do. They never went to fishing parties, prayer meetings, bingo games. They also had nothing to do with the VA hospital, which was a large part of life in our area. They mostly spoke Spanish, but their English was not bad. Corazón's English was actually very good.

Both Corazón and Ray smoked Marlboro Reds and nothing else. Those cigarettes were like a flag to them, like a cigarette nation,

window ledge a shelf below a window; *Fensterbrett*

to tap on sth. to hit sth. gently

swing set *Schaukel*

to sneak (snuck, snuck) to go somewhere secretly

to cast (cast, cast) (*lit.*) to throw sth.

to pledge allegiance to promise to be loyal

to keep a lookout (*phr. v.*) to keep watching what is going on and be careful

to sway to move slowly from side to side

to be fixed up *zurecht gemacht sein*

nightgown *Nachthemd*

gremlin *Kobold*

inflatable *aufblasbar*

punctured without air due to a hole made by a sharp object

previous earlier

tenant *Mieter*

junk things that are considered useless or worthless and thrown away

to negotiate *verhandeln*

to sift through to examine closely

Lay's US brand of potato chips

and they had pledged allegiance. They had cartons all over the place because they brought them back from Mexico, where cigarettes were cheap.

I was only able to get into the Mexicans' trailer on Saturday mornings. On those days, I kept a lookout from the park's recreation area. I could sway gently on the cracked swing and keep a look out to see when Ray left for his job as a gardener. Then I had to wait and see when Corazón left her house to go shopping.

Corazón was always fixed up. We never caught her outside in a nightgown or T-shirt and underwear like everyone else. She never left her trailer without being all made up and her black hair perfectly blown out straight down her back. Corazón's skin was deep brown and her eyes were black. She always wore a deep-red lipstick.

Ray had light brown curly hair and brown eyes. He looked like he could be from anywhere.

Corazón was a Mexican Indian, my mother said with respect. She knows about many things we could never imagine.

Outside Ray and Corazón's trailer, stuck into the muddy grass, were five plastic pink flamingoes and the plastic figure of a gremlin. There was a two-ring inflatable pool in the shape of a turtle that was punctured and lay under a tree and was filled with mud and rotten leaves. Those things must have been left by a previous tenant, as Ray and Corazón did not have children.

Ray had built a large shed on one side of the trailer that contained stacks of newspapers. He also had an old rusty junk of a car without seats inside, which he used to store newspapers and cardboard.

Mrs. Roberta Young thought that Ray, apart from working as a gardener, also worked in the paper recycling business, because he had negotiated buying newspapers straight from the dump trucks. This way he did not have to sift through the dump's piles of garbage looking for paper, although sometimes he did this too.

In the park, Ray and Corazón had the largest mobile home, a triple-wide. So, inside there was even room for a large flat-screen television set, which covered up one of the windows. This meant that it was always dark inside.

My mother and I, curled up in the backseat of the Mercury together, watched movies, shows, and the news on a cheap phone a soldier at the hospital had given to her. Everything we looked at, Mount Everest and the moon, were the size of her hand.

The Mexicans had packs of Snickers bars or Milky Ways on the kitchen counter and had large bags of Lay's barbecue-flavored potato chips lying around. If April May asked me to I'd also steal some of the candy.

Outside the trailer by the door, Corazón had a red plastic bucket full of bottles of nail polish, which she liked to collect.

On the other side of the door there was a large azalea in a pot. Dozens of stubbed-out cigarettes poked out of the soil so the yellow filters looked like weeds growing under the flowers. It just killed me that I couldn't steal these often half-smoked butts, as they were wet and soggy from the dirt.

April May and I often went to the dock to smoke our cigarettes. She was convinced that alligators must be afraid of smoke and would not come near us.

No animal or insect or any living thing likes fires, she said.

Every afternoon, the first question April May asked was how many cigarettes I had managed to steal and then we decided how to divide them up. If we only had one, we would share it back and forth between us counting out the puffs. If I'd managed to steal a pack, we would smoke all the cigarettes.

On those quiet afternoons on the dock, we liked to light up, lie down on our backs, and blow the smoke up at the sky.

April May was a little jealous because I had figured out how to make smoke rings.

It's easy. Just make a big *O* with your mouth, I said.

She never could do it.

I watched the rings of tobacco smoke leave my mouth and rise above me. At first they were tiny but, as they lifted, the smoldering circles expanded and grew wide and full over our bodies and toward the clouds. I knew my smoke rings would be blown out into the ocean, under the clouds, and become great hoops over Italy.

There was another reason April May and I were not that frightened of being down by the river as the alligators were culled every week. This was because every Sunday, after the ten o'clock church services, April May's father and several other men who lived in town liked to go down to the river with a cooler full of beers and their pistols and shotguns. They would drink beer and shoot at the water over and over again just in case there were alligators in there.

I knew there were thousands of bullets in the riverbed. Some had even washed up to the shore and were mixed in with the gravel.

Several times a year the water would deliver a red oily liquid that settled on the top and the men would know they'd hit something.

Every Sunday as my mother and I made peanut butter and jelly sandwiches for lunch in the backseat of the car, we knew the men were shooting.

From the Mercury we could hear the sound of the bullets opening fire on the water.

There they go again, my mother said. They're killing the river.

azalea a type of rhododendron; *Azalee*

weed *Unkraut*

butt *Zigarettenstummel*

to light up to light (and smoke) a cigarette

to smolder to burn slowly without a flame

hoop a ring

to cull to pick out and destroy unwanted animals

cooler *Kühltasche*

gravel *Kieselstein*

8

Everyone at the park was selling something or promising something or dreaming something. No one believed in anything. It didn't take too long to figure it all out.

to figure sth. out to understand sth.

Pastor Rex was giving out prayers and promising to buy a piano for the church. He also bought guns. This new venture made stealing cigarettes more difficult, as there were more people going in and out of the park.

venture new (business) activity that involves risk and danger

I'm getting the guns off the street, he said. I'm helping to stop violence in America. Please bring me your guns – even your old guns that have been around the block.

People in the area soon learned they could sell Pastor Rex their guns if they needed money. Pastor Rex even placed an ad in the local newspaper, which started: 'Give Your Guns to God.'

Because of this, everyone in the park had grown accustomed to men idling through the front gate with a shotgun over a shoulder or a pistol in a pocket. I remember seeing one man carrying a large brown suitcase that must have been full of pistols.

to be accustomed to sth. to be familiar with sth.; *gewöhnt sein an etw.*
to idle ['aɪdəl] to walk slowly

As I made my way around the park there was often one man or two or three sitting on the metal steps leading into Pastor Rex's trailer waiting to sell him their guns. Once in a while, if one of the men smoked, I asked if I could bum a cigarette for my mother. There was a fifty-fifty chance the man would reach into his pack and give me a cigarette.

to bum sth. (*sl.*) to ask sb. for sth. without intending to pay for it; *etw. schnorren*

One old man didn't believe me and said, You're already a little imp and you're never going to grow another inch thanks to your smoking, stupid girl.

imp a small evil spirit; *Kobold*

When I used to complain about my size, my mother liked to tell me stories about Thumbelina. Just think, she said, Thumbelina slept in a matchbox, rested on a carnation leaf, and used a walnut shell as a boat.

Thumbelina a 1994 American animated musical film, based on the fairy tale *Däumelinchen* by Hans Christian Andersen
matchbox *Streichholzschachtel*

Even though I liked the Thumbelina stories, I knew that old man cursed me right then and there. He cast a witch-on-a-broom spell on me. After he told me that I was stupid, he gave me two cigarettes and said, Go on, girl, set yourself on fire. Forever after I knew it was his fault I stayed so small.

to curse sb. to wish evil upon sb.; *jdn. verfluchen*
to cast a spell on sb. to use words thought to be magic in order to have an effect on sb.

The buying of guns was another of Pastor Rex's programs like the U-Turn Prayer and Drive-Thru program. The Give Your Guns to God initiative was supposed to last a month, he'd promised when it started, but it was so successful he decided not to stop. For the time being, he announced at church one morning, he'd continue to do this until the Lord told him not to.

Mrs. Roberta Young complained that she didn't like to have men coming into the trailer park on a regular basis and wanted to start a petition, but no one wanted to have problems with Pastor Rex.

If I went to the church's activities it was almost always with April May, as my mother was raised a Catholic and looked down on any other church. She believed that the Catholic Church was its own land or territory. This was because the same words were spoken, but also because of the scent of incense and candles. Anywhere in the world a Catholic church smelled the same.

I don't believe in their worship, my mother said. And remember, you're going only because of good manners, because April May is inviting you, and not because you like how they love Jesus.

My mother did have to go to Pastor Rex's church on occasion because so many of the events in the community occurred there. Pastor Rex organized bingo games, garage sales, Bible-study groups, Soldier Devotion Worship for the war veterans, and Dancing in the Spirit dance nights.

Ray and Corazón were the only other Catholics in the area. My mother called them Mexican Catholics because they worshipped the Virgin of Guadalupe.

Because Pastor Rex was always helping someone, we were not surprised when he rented out one room in his two-room trailer to a man from Texas. Pastor Rex told Rose about the man and then April May told me and I told my mother. This was usually the way news got around in the park. The truth is Rose knew what was going on at all times because there was always someone who had a headache or a backache. Rose had an enormous bottle of Tylenol, and she'd give out those pills to anyone as if they were jelly beans.

After she placed six Tylenol pills in the palm of his hand, Pastor Rex told Rose about a friend who was staying with him who had fallen on hard times. They'd known each other back home, from a church in Texas. Pastor Rex said the man was going to stay with him for a few months and look around for work.

He's a man fallen, Pastor Rex said. Every man is one wrong turn away from being homeless. There's not much else to know. Every man is one minute away from losing everything.

The first time everyone saw the Texan staying with Pastor Rex was at church at a regular Sunday morning service.

But I'd already seen him.

Late every Wednesday afternoon Pastor Rex went to the veterans' hospital to minister to the sick, and so this was a perfect time after school to check out his trailer for cigarettes to steal.

It was a very hot, humid day. The air seemed to be a cloud that had come down and submerged our trailer park in moisture. In

scent a pleasant natural smell
incense *Weihrauch*

devotion *Andacht*

Virgin of Guadalupe a 1531 legend about the apparition of the Blessed Virgin Mary to an Aztec girl; also: famous painting enshrined in the Basilica of Our Lady of Guadalupe in Mexico City, a popular pilgrimage site

Tylenol medication to treat pain and fever
jelly beans soft sweets

to minister to sb. (*phr. v.*) to give help or care to sb., esp. sb. who is ill
humid *schwül*
to submerge (*lit.*) to cover or hide sth. completely
moisture *Feuchtigkeit*

fan *Ventilator*

orbital motion a path in space around a celestial object

dash the act of running somewhere very quickly
damp slightly wet
to skip to move or hop slightly and quickly

to drizzle *nieseln*

clearing an area in a wood or forest in which trees and bushes have been removed

to lurk to lie in wait
swift *flink*
glide the act of moving easily and gently

this kind of unbearable heat, I knew for certain that most everyone was inside their trailers sitting in front of a fan with a tall cold drink of something.

On this Wednesday afternoon, I was so hot and sleepy, I couldn't even make a fist. Lying in the back of the Mercury trying to stay cool in my underwear and T-shirt, I couldn't even think to do my homework.

Mrs. Roberta Young said these kinds of days made her believe it was true that the Earth was getting closer to the sun.

It's the Earth's orbital motion change, she said.

Land is always in the mind of flying birds, Noelle answered with her fortune-cookie words.

I didn't even bother to dress or put on some shoes when I decided to make a quick dash, a quick cigarette run, to Pastor Rex's trailer. Outside the car, the air felt cool on my skin. The damp grass under my feet was warm. I skipped past the slide and swing set and public bathroom.

By now it had started to drizzle as the heavy air could no longer store the water, so I picked up speed and ran through a small clearing of trees. I slowed down as I circled around the Mexicans' trailer surrounded by broken lawn furniture and the plastic pink flamingos just in case Corazón was outside. No one was around, but dozens of piles of newspapers tied with string near the trailer's front door were getting wet.

Before I hopped up the three steps and opened the door to Pastor Rex's trailer, I looked around to make sure no one was lurking nearby. Then, in a swift glide of a move, I opened the door, stepped in, and slammed the metal door behind me.

Rainwater trickled down my forehead and cheeks. My T-shirt and underwear were plastered to my skin as if the cloth had become my body. I shook my head to get the rain out of my hair.

At that moment, I was not thinking about stealing cigarettes, I was trying to figure out how I was going to keep the tobacco dry. My mind was already focused on finding a plastic supermarket bag or something near the kitchen counter.

What are you doing here, girl? Eli said.

I heard his voice before I saw him.

I stopped. I held my breath. I stopped. I stopped.

What are you doing here, girl?

He spoke the words, all together, as if they were one word: What-are-you-doing-here-girl?

I slowly turned to my left and saw Eli on Pastor Rex's bed.

He sat naked on the edge of the mattress in front of a large round fan. He held a shotgun across his knees.

He did not move to try to hide his nakedness.

I didn't move either. My newfound me, a thief-that-is-caught me, didn't answer.

A yearning to get out of the rain, huh? he said. His voice was soft and musical as if speaking were a song.

I nodded. I could hear drum thunder in me and outside.

His eyes were blue, really blue, and not like the sky or ocean or other blue things that I could think of. He had long black hair.

Hey girl, turn and face the door, he said.

I knew what he could see. His eyes held a small girl who was so white she could have been a peeled apple, a baby bottle of milk, a scoop of vanilla ice cream. He looked at my new body that was moving across the line from twelve to thirteen.

You're as white as a candle, little girl. I bet there's a wick that can be lit up inside of you, he said.

I didn't move. I didn't understand.

Hey, girl, turn and face the door. Turn around. Turn your pretty self around. Let me get some denims on. And then I'll fix you a towel so you can dry off.

I did turn around.

I spun around.

I opened the door, ran down the steps, past the Mexicans, the old slide and swing set, and zigzagged through the trailers until I got to the Mercury. I yanked the door open, jumped in, pulled the heavy car door closed, threw myself down on the floor under the glove compartment, and rolled myself into a little ball of a girl.

the line from twelve to thirteen reference to a song from the 1985 musical *A Chorus Line* about the experiences of growing up and becoming an adult; here: being in puberty and becoming a teenager
wick *Kerzendocht*

to spin (spun, spun) around to turn rapidly

9

The second time I saw Eli, I was with April May and her parents at church. Mrs. Roberta Young was across the aisle from us with Noelle. They were both dressed up in white and looked very serious with their hands folded in their laps. My mother thought they were the last people on Earth to dress up for God. Everyone else in the building was dressed in regular jeans, shorts, and T-shirts. It really horrified my mother and contributed to her disdain for Protestants.

aisle *Gang*

to horrify to produce a reaction of distaste

disdain *Verachtung*

At the very back of the building several of the benches were reserved for the wounded men and nurses who came from the VA hospital. Every Sunday there was a bus service that would bring the war veterans to church. Some of the men were in wheelchairs and others moved on crutches. Nurses came with them to help those who couldn't walk well or to push wheelchairs. Sometimes, if Rose was on duty, she'd sit in the back with the vets. A strong male nurse carried one man, who had no legs or arms, into the church every Sunday.

to be on duty *im Dienst sein*

Rose said the veterans' hospital had every kind of man in it.

When I looked at the men at the back of the church on those mornings I knew she was right. There were men back there of every shape and color.

Rose said, The war wounded are a storybook.

Eli walked in after the congregation was already seated. His black cowboy boots rang out on the floor. He wore blue jeans and a clean white shirt.

congregation *Kirchengemeinde*

to ring (rang, rung) out (*phr. v.*) *ertönen:* here: *hervorstechen*

He also had a shotgun slung over each shoulder.

Rose poked Sergeant Bob with her elbow and whispered, Who's this man? Can you open carry in church?

to open carry (*US*) to carry a gun in a way that people can see it

Everyone looked at him.

Eli nodded slightly to the people on his left and right as he strode toward the front of the church.

to stride (strode, stridden) *schreiten, stolzieren*

Rose said, That man walks down the aisle like he thinks he's the bride.

When he saw me sitting in a pew to his left like a small white egg, he closed his eyes for just a second, both of them. It was his way of saying, I know you.

When he reached the front pew he pulled one shotgun strap from one shoulder and then drew the other off and laid them both on the bench and sat down.

Later when I told my mother about Eli, she said, There is only one kind of man who carries two shotguns into church. That's a man who doesn't turn the other cheek.

to turn the other cheek reference to the Bible; not to do anything to hurt sb. who has hurt you

Eli took in a deep breath. We all watched him. Everyone in that church could both feel and see his breath because he didn't yet know that in our slice of Florida he had to breathe shallow. He didn't yet know that the fumes from the dump and the murky and diseased, alligator-infested river could make him sick. He breathed deep as if he didn't know mosquitoes were breeding everywhere and that hurricane season was only a week away. He breathed deep as if the church air could fill him with amens.

A scent of lemon mixed with pinecones followed him into the church.

That was perfume, Sergeant Bob said. Girl perfume.

April May squeezed my arm and looked at me and crossed her eyes. She always crossed her eyes when she wanted to say, This is messed up.

Across from where I was sitting, I could see Noelle and Mrs. Roberta Young. Noelle had two Barbie dolls with long yellow hair sticking out of the front pocket of her jeans. I could see that Noelle's ankle-length socks had lost their elastic and had slipped down into her shoes. The socks were rumpled up in folds and no longer covered her heels. Noelle didn't seem to notice.

We heard the story about Eli in a sermon that Pastor Rex gave that very morning with the man looking up at him from the front pew.

Pastor Rex wiped his brow with a light-blue handkerchief and began the sermon. He said, I'm not going to talk about our Lord Jesus, I'm going to talk about my friend from Texas, Mr. Eli Redmond.

When Pastor Rex said the word 'Eli,' I did not know yet that we were in trouble. I did not know that my mother was this man's deer to hunt and that his name would be the song inside her body. Later my mother would say that this was no coincidence. Billie Holiday had sent Eli Redmond to her. Bessie Smith and Nina Simone had shepherded him there. Etta James was singing 'At Last.' My mother didn't believe in coincidence, she believed in divine intervention.

April May listened to the sermon and turned to me and crossed her eyes again. She was not buying any of this.

Eli Redmond is a man among us who has fallen on hard times, Pastor Rex said.

I looked at Eli. I could see his profile. He smiled as Pastor Rex talked about him and leaned back against the hard wood bench and crossed his arms. He liked hearing the story of his life.

Eli Redmond had lost his family, Pastor Rex repeated. He lost his family just as if his house were the *Mary Celeste*. Do you remember that boat? That was one sad story. It was found on the sea

slice here: small piece
to breathe shallow *flach atmen*
fumes strong, unpleasant and sometimes dangerous gas or smoke
murky dark and dirty
mosquitoes *Mücken*

pinecone *Pinienzapfen*

rumpled up not smooth, untidy
fold *Falte*

deer *Rotwild; Reh*
coincidence *Zufall*
Billie Holiday (1915 – 1959) African-American jazz singer; known for her improvisational skills; suffered from drug and alcohol abuse and abusive relationships
Bessie Smith (1894 – 1937) African-American blues singer, known for her rough behaviour
Nina Simone (1933 – 2003) African-American singer, pianist and civil rights activist
to shepherd to make sb. move where you want them to go
Etta James (1938 – 2012) African-American singer; she won six Grammy awards
divine *göttlich*
intervention *Fügung*
to buy sth. (*infml.*) to believe sth.
to fall on hard times to lose your money and start to have a difficult life

with the mashed potatoes and ham still hot on the plates and not a soul on board. Not a soul. People never knew what happened to that boat, but it must have been bad. Bad. The lifeboat was still attached. How did these people disappear? Where did they go? This is one of the ocean's great mysteries.

Well, Eli came home to his house from work and his wife and two boys were gone, Pastor Rex said.

to swivel *sich (um-)drehen*

Everyone in the church turned, swiveled, or leaned forward to look at the man from Texas. Now his head was bowed and his eyes were closed as if his own eyes could not stand to hear his own story.

hasn't had no luck (*infml.*) to be unsuccessful

Yes, indeed, Pastor Rex said, this is a man who lost everything. His family disappeared, went missing, vanished. He's looked for them but hasn't had no luck. I hope his bad luck will be good luck as the loving family of our church takes him in. We can be his lifeboats.

Noelle had put down her Bible and had taken her Barbie dolls out of her pocket. She was holding them in her hands and making them walk on their tiptoe-shaped plastic feet along the back of the pew.

mold *Schimmel*

I looked around the church. The church's ceiling was covered with patches of mold. There was a large image of Jesus in a frame on the left wall and a simple metal cross on the right wall. I didn't want to focus on Pastor Rex, who had now turned bright red with emotion as he repeated, Oh yes, lifeboats, yes, this is what we must be. Lifeboats. Who will carry the life vest for this man? He cannot drink saltwater. It's like it says in the famous poem. So, who will bring him fresh water? Who will give him work to do? When Pastor Rex said, Do not kill the albatross, everyone in the church grew still.

life vest *Rettungsweste*

Who will bring him fresh water? … Do not kill the albatross. reference to the famous ballad *The Rime of the Ancient Mariner* by Samuel Taylor Coleridge (1772 – 1834) about a ship getting caught in a bad storm; an albatross appears and leads the crew out of the storm but the angry mariner shoots the bird

April May turned to me and whispered, Albatross? What?

The Lord be with you all, Pastor Rex said. And to finish, let us pray.

At this in the service some people stood up from their pews while others got down on their knees.

to kneel (knelt, knelt) *knien*

I knelt next to April May. Sergeant Bob struggled down and also knelt on his one knee beside me while Rose continued to stand.

I closed my eyes tightly and prayed to God and thanked him for the Catholic fact that my mother was not in the Protestant church to hear about Eli Redmond. I knew she'd be thinking about touching his forehead and placing a thermometer in his mouth.

At the end of the prayer, Pastor Rex asked Eli Redmond to stand and say a few words.

rockabye-baby a 2006 series of instrumental lullaby song versions of songs by famous bands including the Beatles and the Rolling Stones

Eli stood up and turned around to look at the congregation, and for the second time I heard his rockabye-baby voice.

He said,Like a tree alone in a field, I stand here. No other trees are helping me to bear the wind and storm. Lightning struck this tree, struck me. I want to find my woman and my brood. I can't slumber in the day or night. There is no repose for my eyes that don't see their eyes. You can dandy up your imagination, but nothing can prepare you for this.

Eli spoke as if he were bent over a cradle.

No one is loving me, he said, and then he was almost really singing. Maybe my woman is calling to me. Maybe they're walking along a highway. Maybe they're in that dwelling where no one comes back from. Maybe.

Everyone was quiet. For one day the word 'maybe' became the most important word of our lives. It was a word we'd never given a place to on the mantelpiece of words and now it sounded like a word that contained answers.

Behind me, in the pews at the back, I could hear the war veterans' breath exit and enter their bodies with deliberation, as if they were counting the chime of the day's new word: maybe, maybe, maybe.

The men tried hard not to stare at Eli Redmond, but they could not stop because they knew him, because they'd been like him so long ago.

They looked at the Texan and remembered what it had been like to hold a woman by the waist and squeeze her just a little so she'd feel their strength in her body.

I could hear the restless sound of metal crutches slip and fall and the whine and wheeze of wheelchairs as they stirred in place.

The broken soldiers knew they were ruins as they looked upon this man.

lightning *Blitz*

brood young children
to slumber (*lit.*) to sleep
repose rest
to dandy sth. up to make sth. look stylish and fashionable

cradle *Wiege*

dwelling (*fml.*) a house or place to live in

with deliberation (*fml.*) not impulsive but with intention
chime a ringing sound; *Glockenton*

whine and wheeze *Schnaufen und Jammern*
to stir to move

10

My mother was so good, she was too good.
Some people would say that kind of goodness needed to be locked up.
She never said no to me.
I'm like a cup of sugar, she liked to say. You can borrow me anytime.
She was a cup of sugar.
But sweetness is always looking for Mr. Bad and Mr. Bad can pick out Miss Sweet in any crowd – just like magnets. Mr. Bad was the refrigerator and Miss Sweet was the *Florida Loves Oranges* magnet sticking to the door.
My mother invited Eli Redmond into our car to visit.
She opened her mouth in a great wide *O* and breathed him tight into her body.
She opened her mouth and breathed in the balm and musk of Eli Redmond.
I could not understand. She knew all the songs, so why would she get messed and stirred up with a man like this?
And she knew all the love songs that are a university for love. She knew the 'I'm So Lonely I Ain't Even High' and 'Call Me Anything But Call Me' songs.
When he said his name was Eli she was down on her knees.
His voice tamed her immediately. The first word of love he said was all she needed. He said, *I'm your medicine sweet baby my oh my your name has always been written on my heart.*
And thereafter all he had to do was whistle for her.
My mother and Eli met for the first time in the dilapidated recreation area we passed on the way to the bathroom.
Every morning our routine was to get out of the Mercury early and go to the bathroom. I always went in first while my mother waited for me outside.
On the day my mother met Eli Redmond, I was in the small bathroom washing my face and brushing my teeth when I heard voices outside. It was my mother talking to the Texan. I knew it was Eli because he was singing every word.
He said, What do you mean? You knew I was coming? Like the spring?
Yes.
When I came out of the bathroom, I found my mother sitting on the cracked plastic swing in her long, almost transparent, lavender-colored nightgown. Eli stood behind her and was propelling her small body into the air.

balm *Balsam*
musk *Moschus*
ain't (*sl.*) am not
to propel [prəˈpel] to push or move sb. fast

He held a burning cigarette tight between his teeth so that he could use both hands to push her into the morning sky. My mother's eyes were closed so she could feel his hands against her lower back and hips.

I walked back to the Mercury alone and began to dress for school. About half an hour later my mother came back. She opened the door and crawled onto the backseat. She turned around and lay down on her back and placed her hands over her face as if she didn't want Eli's face to leave her eyes. Her bare feet were muddy. Somewhere on her morning voyage from the bathroom to our car she'd lost her flip-flops.

Baby, Pearl, she said. I believe in love at first sight. Be careful what you look at.

From then on my mother was always staring into her wishing-well watch. In the round face of hours and minutes she looked for time to spend with Eli.

Maybe I'm getting my future back, she said.

The following Sunday my mother pushed me out of the Mercury and told me to go to church with April May. She told me to go off in kind, soft words, but they might have been a soldier's hard combat boot giving me a kick. She wanted to be alone with Eli.

A week had gone by with Eli trying to bribe me out of the car with candy. He brought a yellow packet of peanut M&M's and a bag of jelly beans. But he read me fast. It took him only two days to figure out that what I really wanted was a cigarette. Thanks to my mother's burning up for Eli, April May and I could count on a regular supply of Camels.

The following Sunday there was a sense of expectation in the church. Even Pastor Rex kept looking over his shoulder to the front door as he set up the altar. The soldiers shifted and looked around. The women were more groomed than usual and a few men were wearing long-sleeved shirts, which was pretty unheard-of.

The congregation was waiting for Eli, but I knew he was with my mother in the backseat of our car.

So much for Eli's missing family, April May whispered to me.

Yes.

So, your mother and Eli have gone the sweetheart way?

Yes.

Salt meet wound, she said.

Pastor Rex became unraveled as he went through the routine of the church service. In his sermon he talked about the Miracle of the Mule and the Miracle of the Miser's Heart, but it was hard to follow what he was trying to say. His hands trembled as he held the prayer book.

combat boot *Kampfstiefel*
to bribe sb. *jdn. bestechen*
supply *Nachschub*
groomed *gepflegt, herausgeputzt*
to unravel to explain a mystery
the Miracle of the Mule biblical story about the conversion of a heretic (*Ketzer*)
the Miracle of the Miser's Heart biblical story about a heartless miser (*Geizhals*)
to tremble *zittern*

I looked over at the pew where Noelle and her mother were sitting. Noelle looked as if she hadn't brushed her hair all week. She was wearing a deep-red lipstick.

Look at Noelle, April May said. Look at her.

She must have put her finger in the electrical socket, I said.

April May nodded.

miracle *Wunder*

Pastor Rex finished his sermon and said, So, this is my question for all of us today. Do we believe in miracles? Everyone here needs to ask themselves this question. Do you believe in miracles? Then ask yourself, if you don't believe in miracles, how can you ask for one?

to faint *ohnmächtig werden*

At these words, I watched Noelle slip down from the pew and onto the floor. She'd fainted.

scramble act of hurrying

There was a scramble as a few people ran to help Mrs. Roberta Young lift Noelle and lay her down on the bench. Rose left our side and quickly went over to take Noelle's pulse. Pastor Rex raced down from the altar to see if he could help.

As Rose felt Noelle's forehead for fever, Pastor Rex used his prayer book to fan Noelle's face.

departure leaving

At this point, everyone realized that the service was over and began to leave the building. It was a quiet departure as if a baby were asleep or there'd been a death.

Sergeant Bob, April May, and I sat in the pew and waited for Rose to finish nursing Noelle.

The diagnosis was easy.

Noelle had also fallen in love with Eli Redmond. The moment he'd walked down the aisle she knew it and she'd been fainting ever since.

We learned that, after the previous church service when Eli had been introduced to the congregation, Noelle had gone home to do some gardening. It took her several hours to dig holes all around the trailer. She used two large spoons and a fork from the kitchen as gardening tools.

When Noelle had finished digging sixty-three holes, she carried her large collection of Barbie dolls outside and one by one stuck each doll in one hole. She planted the dolls in feet first and only up to the dolls' knees.

petal *Blütenblatt*

The rows of Barbies surrounding her trailer looked like a field of dolls. From a distance, for a second, the yellow, red, black, and brown doll hair looked like bruised petals.

sth. is kicking dust (*sl.*) sth. bad is about to happen

When I walked over to Noelle's trailer for a math class only two days after the arrival of Eli and saw the field of dolls, I knew something was kicking dust. I also knew the moment April May saw this doll landscape she'd be talking about it for the next two weeks.

I walked up the two steps of the trailer and peered in to see if anyone was home. Through the screen door I could see Noelle lying down on the sofa reading a book. I had never seen her read. Mrs. Roberta Young read all the time and always had books lying around, but I didn't think Noelle was capable of doing this.

Noelle was dressed in a long, flowing pink nightgown. It was exactly the same as my mother's lavender nightgown. Noelle and my mother had bought the same princess nightie at Walmart, where it came in lavender, pink, and orange for nine dollars and ninety-five cents and was fireproof.

I knew there was not going to be a math class.

Next to Noelle there was a Wizard of Oz-green pack of Salem cigarettes. I decided to go in and talk to her and see if I could steal a cigarette or two. The taste of mint smoke was already in my mouth. But before doing this, I walked back to the field of dolls and, grabbing them by their heads, I pulled five of them out of the ground like weeds. I left them lying on the damp earth.

I walked back to the trailer and knocked on the frame of the screen door. Noelle looked up, sat up, and then walked to the door. She almost seemed to float in the silky nightgown.

Through the door's screen netting she could see me.

Oh, it's you, Pearl, she said. What do you want?

May I come in? I said.

Noelle opened the door.

Over my shoulder she could see the dolls I'd pulled out of the ground.

Oh no! she said, and pushed past me to the doll garden.

I entered the trailer and slipped two Salems out of the pack and up my sleeve.

I knew what had happened to Noelle. When she saw Eli for the first time at church, he'd turned her into a woman. Noelle had not closed her mouth. Noelle had swallowed him.

Mrs. Roberta Young hated Eli Redmond from the moment she saw him walk down the aisle.

In fact, Mrs. Roberta Young wanted to borrow Sergeant Bob's lie detector machine. She called it a polygraph. Sergeant Bob used it for fishing tournaments as people were always cheating and lying about their catch.

Nobody can beat the box, Sergeant Bob said.

He made money on the side traveling around Florida and conducting lie detector tests at the state tournaments. He called this purity fishing. He said the contestants had to sign an agreement to take the test before they could participate in the fishing tournament.

Walmart an American multinational chain of hypermarkets

Wizard of Oz a 1939 American musical fantasy film based on a children's book, with the Wizard wearing a frog-green costume

weeds *Unkraut*

tournament *Wettbewerb*

to conduct sth. to carry sth. out

purity the quality of having good morals and a good character

contestant *Wettkämpfer, Kandidat*

Sergeant Bob was always working on new questions. The standard questions he asked were, Did you take any fish from anyone outside your boat? Did you hide any fish in your boat or truck? Did you take any fish out off a caged area? Did you ever lie about your fish to get out of trouble?

Rose dreaded that machine. She knew that her husband would hook her up to it in a second if he thought she might be cheating on him. So, she knew she never could, not even in her imagination.

Sergeant Bob used to tell all his fishermen friends that he'd do the lie detector on their wives for free. He laughed and said, Just replace the word 'fish' with the word 'lover' and it works!

The machine is like a Supreme Court judge sitting in the corner of my bedroom, Rose said to my mother one day at the hospital.

Sergeant Bob explained how some people would put a sharp tack in their shoe and press their foot down on it when they were telling the truth. The truth-trickers thought that feeling pain while telling the truth would look just like the anxiety of telling a lie.

Mrs. Roberta Young wished she could try the machine out on Eli, but she couldn't think of a scheme to get it done.

She said, Eli Redmond is the breeze that makes a hurricane from the Atlantic. He's a purebred liar. He's that kind of man who breaks all the windows in your house.

to dread sth. [dred] to feel extremely worried about or afraid of sth.

to hook sb. up to sth. to connect or fasten sb. to sth.

Supreme Court judge a judge working in the most important law court in the US

tack *Reißzwecke*

anxiety [æŋˈzaɪəti] a feeling of nervousness and worry

scheme plan of action

purebred with parents that are both of the same breed; *reinrassig*; here: *echt*

11

Eli took over my place.

He kicked me right out of the car.

Eli kept his Texas cowboy boots outside near the front left tire. He threw his jeans jacket across the hood and propped his sunglasses on one of the windshield wipers.

He never knocked.

My mother felt his footsteps from far away. We could be singing, or eating something, or she'd be helping me with my homework and she'd suddenly look up and stop whatever we were doing. She'd smooth down her frizzy yellow hair and pop a sugar cube in her mouth.

And sure enough, in a few minutes, I'd look out the window and Eli would be walking toward us. He'd be looking at the sky. I don't know why he never tripped on anything or took a stepped-on-a-crack kind of step. He looked up at the sky and the ground didn't care.

Run off and play. Off you go. Go find yourself something to do. Off with you, my mother said.

As I got out on one side of the car, Eli would slide in on the other. He always went straight for the backseat, as if it were a bed.

Run off and play, my mother said.

I would leave and go into the park, but I really had nowhere to go. Sometimes I was lucky and could hang out with April May, but most of the time I just wandered over to the recreation area and sat on the swing for an hour or two until I spied Eli leaving the Mercury and heading back to Pastor Rex's trailer.

Once in a while I went down to the river, but I was afraid to be down there by myself because of the alligators.

I never went to the dump either. It was one thing to find a rotten carcass of a dog with April May and another to find one all alone. The last time we'd been to the dump April May found a plastic bag full of dry shredded snakeskins. I found a bullet complete with a brass jacket inside a bottle of wine. The bullet shone inside the glass and I had to break the bottle to get it out. Scratched crudely into one side of the bullet were the letters *V* and *P*.

My, my, April May said, that bullet had someone's name on it.

I don't think it was ever used.

Take it with you. There's still time to use it.

Of course. I'm not leaving it here, I said, and placed the genie-bullet-in-the-bottle in the pocket of my jeans.

After a few days of wandering around the park with no place to go, I realized that Eli was going to spend every moment my mother was home from work in our car.

hood *Motorhaube*

to trip on sth. *über etw. stolpern*

stepped-on-a-crack reference to a children's game called 'step on a crack, break your mother's back', in which anyone who steps on the cracks between the paving stones is out until only one player is left

genie ['dʒi:ni] *Flaschengeist*

Now the Mercury even smelled like him when he wasn't there. It was Brut cologne, my mother said. I told April May about the Brut and she told Rose, who said that was the cologne Elvis Presley always used.

There was one abandoned trailer in the back of the park. The last tenants were a young wife and her two-year-old child. The woman's husband had been badly wounded in Iraq and had been treated at the VA hospital. I knew the soldier had died from his injuries and that the wife had left and gone back to live with her parents in Tampa.

Now that Eli was always in my car, I checked out the empty trailer. I was weary of wandering the park with nowhere to go, and needed a place to do my homework and get away from the mosquitoes.

The trailer was clean. There were some trailer homes that were elaborate and even had rooms, but this one was very simple. It was just one very long and narrow room. On one side there was a kitchen, small bathroom with a shower, and a counter table with two stools that were left behind.

On the other side of the trailer there was a narrow bunk bed. The top bunk was just an empty frame, but the bottom bed still had an old mattress on it. There was graffiti on the wood headboard. Carved with a thin pen knife or paring knife were the words: *I'm waiting for Halley's Comet 2061.*

Left behind on the floor was a children's book and a toy truck. The book was a coloring book, which contained drawings of pistols, shotguns, rifles, and machine guns. The cover read *Gun Coloring Book.*

In the kitchen drawers I found a pack of gauze bandages and a hunting knife with a long whitish-yellow handle and a coffee cup full of fishing flies. The coffee cup had a photograph of a whale on one side and the words *SeaWorld Orlando* on the other.

Under the sink there were two unopened boxes of large black garbage bags and a toilet plunger.

In the bathroom there was a bar of green Zest soap that was still in its wrapping and a stained towel hanging on the back of the door.

As days turned to weeks my time in the empty trailer became routine as Eli went to the Mercury almost every afternoon and left late, only when it was my bedtime.

My mother never asked where I went or what I was doing. I watched as her love for Eli made her sleepy. It was hard for her to get up and get ready for work.

She had a few explanations for her sleepiness.

I have too many questions running around inside, she said. This does not let me sleep.

to abandon to give up

Iraq Iraq War (2003 – 2011), armed conflict that overthrew the dictator Saddam Hussein

Tampa major city on the west coast of Florida

weary ['wɪəri] very tired, unwilling

elaborate containing a lot of detail

bunk bed *Etagenbett*

to carve *schnitzen*
pen knife *Taschenmesser*
paring knife *Schälmesser*
Halley's Comet a comet visible from Earth every 75 years
coloring book *Malbuch*

gauze *Verbandmull*

toilet plunger *Toilettensaugglocke*
Zest an American brand of soap and body wash products

What kind of questions, I asked.

Every kind, she said. Do animals speak to each other? Do we have to keep a promise after someone dies? You know. Those kinds of questions. Will my life matter? And I even ask myself if Mr. Don't Come Back will come back. I'm missing him.

One evening when I left the empty trailer to go home for bedtime, I came across Pastor Rex. He was standing very still behind the entrance gate to the park, where he was hidden from view behind a tree. He gazed over toward the visitors' parking area and our car. From this spot he could see that my mother was sitting in the backseat on Eli's lap.

I knew Eli was sitting in the exact spot Pastor Rex expected would be his place. Before the day Eli came to live with him, Pastor Rex had imagined he would be decorating the backseat of the Mercury with his own stuff.

He had not seen me or heard me approach, so I stepped back a few paces into the shadow of a tree. I was so small it was always easy for me to disappear.

I watched Pastor Rex reach into his jacket pocket and take out a pack of Marlboros and a lighter. He lit up a cigarette and smoked it slowly as he watched my mother and Eli. He smoked as if he were smoking out all the hope. He took in a deep drag, in and in and in, but didn't exhale any smoke. He smoked a whole cigarette in this way. Pastor Rex watched, and I watched, as Eli took off my mother's blouse. He watched, and I watched, as Eli bent down and kissed my mother's small breasts. He watched, and I watched, my mother kiss Eli's face.

When Pastor Rex finished smoking up all his hope, he threw the butt down on the ground, crushed it into the gravel with the heel of his shoe, and turned around and walked back to his trailer in a hurry.

I also turned and went back to my empty trailer for another hour. There was nothing else for me to do.

Now that my mother was loving Eli, she was tasting him deep and only getting a wishing-well kind of hunger. She'd never be full again.

When Eli left and I was back in the car, I watched as she licked the inside of her palms for his taste like a kitten.

At night she slept wearing one of Eli's shirts and moved around fretfully in her sleep.

If my mother had watched another woman in this condition, she would have had the diagnosis in a second. My mother would have said, Pearl, it's like that song – she's askin' for water, but he's givin' her gasoline.

to approach sb. to come near to sb.
pace a single step

drag *Zug*
to exhale ausatmen

blouse [blaʊz]

fretfully *unruhig, ängstlich*

12

When April May and I walked home from school along the highway, we always had our eyes fixed to the side of the road in case there was something interesting on the ground. Once we found a five-dollar bill.

It was on the day that April May and I didn't find any money, but found a small baby raccoon under a bush, that the police stopped at the trailer park to investigate our car.

raccoon *Waschbär*

April May leaned over and looked at the creature closely. It's a baby, she said. Do you think it's wounded? Maybe it's sick.

Just leave it alone, I said. They can have rabies.

rabies ['reɪbi:z] *Tollwut*

Oh, yes, of course, she said, and moved away quickly.

We both picked up our stride as if just being close to the raccoon could make us sick. As we turned toward the trailer park we could see a police car stopped next to the Mercury. The siren was off, but the vehicle's red warning lights blinked and flashed.

My mother stood outside. She was dressed in her lavender nightgown and was barefoot. I knew she must have been asleep when the policemen drove in, and knocked on our car door. The towels we used over the Mercury's windows were still in place. She should have been at work and not in our car. School was out. It was at least three o'clock. She shouldn't have been asleep.

My mother hugged her stomach and rocked back and forth.

There were two policemen with her and both were tall men, which made my mother look even smaller than usual. One had red hair and was covered with freckles. He could have been April May's relative. The other policeman had black hair and dark skin and stood back from the Mercury with his hand on his gun.

The policeman with red hair was walking around the car. He was attempting to peer into the windows through the towels. I heard him say, So, there's no one else in the vehicle, is this correct, lady?

As I walked toward my mother, both men stared at me.

The policeman with black hair let out a sigh. I was used to those looks of astonishment at my eggshell skin and light pastel-blue eyes.

I walked over to my mother and placed my hand in her hand.

The policeman with red hair stepped close to me and said, Hey, are you a real albino?

April May just kept on walking. She looked straight ahead as if she didn't know us.

Is this your daughter? the policeman with red hair asked my mother. He was the only one of the two men who spoke, and he had a cold, clear voice.

I answered for her. Yes, I said, she's my mother.

Do you live in the car? Really?

Yes.

Where's your birth certificate?

The policeman with black hair watched everything as he chewed a piece of gum wedged tightly between his two front teeth. He kept his right hand on the pistol holder at his waist.

to wedge *einklemmen*

Come on, lady. Is this child yours? the policeman asked. Don't tell me you just screwed around like an animal and had a child without even a birth certificate? Jesus! Is she an albino? Does she have a name?

to screw around (*offensive*) to have sex with a lot of people

Pearl. Her name is Pearl, my mother said.

And what about a last name?

France.

And your name?

Margot France.

Do you have the registration for this car? Insurance? Where did you get this? Is it stolen property? Where did you get this car, lady? How long have you been hanging out here?

It's just a junk, really, my mother answered.

Look at all the bags, the other policeman said. He spoke up for the first time as he peered into the window of the Mercury. His voice was a high-pitched, womanly voice. She's like a goddam bag lady, he said.

goddam *(coll.) verflucht*

Hey, Torres, the red-haired policeman said, check out the trunk.

Torres opened the door on the driver's side and flipped the lever for the trunk. Then he walked to the back of the car and looked in.

lever *Hebel*

The beautiful boxes made of cardboard lined with white paper, wood boxes, and leather boxes with fine gold latches were all in place.

latch *Verschluss, Riegel*

He lifted the green felt bag, pulled open the tie, and took out the elephant-tusk boat.

Where did you get this? he asked as he held it in his hands with care.

He placed the ivory boat back in the long bag and lay it back down in the trunk. Then he touched the black leather violin case. He didn't open it.

My God, he said. What is all of this? Did you rob an antique store, lady?

He even lifted and shook the long, flat box, which was lined on the outside in raw silk and wrapped with a yellow silk ribbon.

He looked at the cooler and opened the tap and said, Milk and yoghurt. A Diet Coke. A few apples.

tap *Drehverschluss*

Look at this stuff, Torres said to the other policeman. Come look. Where did you get these things? Did you steal all this?

No, my mother answered. They're things that belonged to my family.

Yeah, right, Torres answered. Let me see your arms.

What do you mean?

My mother's arms were crossed over her breasts.

No. Why?

I won't say it again, Torres said.

wrist *Handgelenk*

He took my mother's left wrist and twisted her arm open to the sunlight.

He looked at the inside of my mother's smooth, soft arm.

tar (*sl.*) not very pure heroin

Well, I thought she might be a user, Torres said. I thought someone might be giving you some tar, lady.

Then Torres turned and looked at me.

What's this pretty little angel of a daughter you have here thinking? Huh? he said.

Listen to me, lady, the redheaded policeman said. He had to lean over at his waist almost a complete right angle in order to look straight into my mother's face.

tow truck *Abschleppwagen*

Listen to me, lady, he said again. We're going to order up a tow truck to take this car away. What are you going to do with your stuff? You better find a place to store it. Once I order up a tow truck to take this car away, it'll be a day or two. Do you have a place to keep your stuff? Where're you going to live?

to meander here: to roll down in curves

My mother began to cry but she didn't make a noise. Her tears just blinked out of her eyes and meandered down her cheeks.

It's not illegal to be homeless, she said. It's not a crime.

She's always been my mother, I said. Ever since the beginning.

Listen, little girl, the policeman answered. If she can't prove it, you're going to go straight into foster care. That's the law. How do we know, she didn't kidnap you, huh? How do I know you're not missing? Maybe you're missing. Maybe.

My mother kept nervously placing one bare foot over the other as if the ground were burning the soles of her feet.

Don't you have a birth certificate? The policeman said. Listen, lady, you cannot live in a car. You're homeless. A car is not a home.

peg leg *Holzbein*

I raised my eyes from my mother's small feet and looked up to see Sergeant Bob limping toward us. He was wearing Bermuda shorts and I could see the place where his peg leg was attached to the stump with a leather strap.

Sergeant Bob had his soldier helmet on his head and was carrying a huge gun on his shoulder. He was ready to fire. I'd once seen the machine gun in his trailer.

April May was running behind him. I thought she'd left us alone to deal with the policemen, and I didn't blame her. Anyone with any intelligence ran away from the police. Instead, she'd run to get help. As I looked at her walking behind her father like a foot soldier, I knew I'd let her boss me around forever. I was hers.

The policemen couldn't see Sergeant Bob as he came up behind them and pointed the gun at the officers.

I don't want to shoot, Sergeant Bob said. I'm not in the mood. Believe me, I know better than to miss. I'm a dead shot.

dead shot *todsicherer Schütze*

The policemen turned around slowly and I could see both the shock and fear in their eyes as they raised their heads.

Hey, hey, the policeman with the red hair said. Slow down, brother.

I'm not your brother.

You know what I mean, man.

I'm not your brother. Get out of here. Both of you. Are you listening to me?

The policeman stepped slowly backward toward the police car.

If you have ownership on your life I'd just turn a circle, walk out of here, and forget this ever happened, Sergeant Bob said. Find yourselves some amnesia.

amnesia a medical condition that makes you unable to remember things

We'll have you arrested, Torres said. You're under arrest now.

Listen, boy, give me your driver's license so I know your name for the rest of my life. If you ever tell about this I will hunt you down and kill your family. I'm PTSD. You know what I mean, right? I'm not responsible. I'm in Kabul right now. The Taliban is walking up the street.

PTSD (*abbr.*) (suffering from) post-traumatic stress disorder
Kabul capital of Afghanistan
Taliban an Islamic fundamentalist movement and military organization

Come on, let's get out of here, the policeman with the red hair said.

That's the spirit, Sergeant Bob answered.

Okay, we're leaving, Torres said, but before he got back into his police car, he turned toward my mother. Listen, lady, he said. You'd better move out of that car or they're going to take your daughter away. It's going to happen.

I want to see the back of your head now, Sergeant Bob said. Get out. You never had this memory.

The cops got into their car and drove away.

Sergeant Bob dropped his shotgun from his shoulder and limped over to my mother. She was so small beside him. He held his weapon in one hand and placed his other hand on my mother's head as if she were a kid.

Listen, he said. Margot, you can't live in this car anymore. You've got to find another place for you and Pearl. Social Services are going to take her away from you and you know it.

Social Services *Sozialfürsorge*

Thank you, Sergeant Bob, my mother said. You're a friend.

I mean it. You have to find a place to live.

I know. I know. Didn't you go to the hospital today?

I forgot.

Margot, you can't forget to go to work. What's up with that?

I just forgot today was Monday, my mother said. I thought it was Sunday.

Sergeant Bob shook his head, turned, and limped back toward his trailer. April May looked at me and shook her head. She looked sad. I knew exactly what she was going to say to me later on. April May's superstition would explain that everything bad that happened was because we'd left that box, with the collection of moths in tissue paper, in the dump.

Through the smoke of a few stolen cigarettes, she was going to say, I told you so. Everything is connected. The police came here because of the moths and their moth souls.

My mother opened the door and got back in the Mercury. I followed her into the backseat. There was a yellow box of Cheerios on the floor. She picked it up, placed it on her lap, and began eating them dry, one by one.

You didn't go to work today? Why not?

I couldn't see myself there, she said.

Why not?

Oh baby, she said. There's a man who they brought in to the hospital a few weeks ago and I just can't look at him. I can't be near him. His wings were torn off. They brought him over here straight from a VA hospital in Miami. They're overcrowded down there. I just can't be at the hospital anymore.

wing here: arm

Why, what's wrong with him?

Baby, he counts his heartbeats.

Maybe, he'll be gone soon, I said.

My mother placed her arm around me. Get cozy with me, she said.

cozy comfortable and pleasant

It's too hot.

Hot? I feel so cold.

Do you think Sergeant Bob scared those policemen away for good?

for good permanently

You know, my mother said. I just had a thought. For all this time, I always thought that Sergeant Bob was KKK. But maybe he isn't. Maybe I was wrong.

KKK (*abbr.*) Ku Klux Klan, an American white supremacist hate group founded in 1865

Two weeks later a gun came into our car. For twelve years the Mercury had been full of dolls, stuffed animals, our clothes, boxes of dried foods and fruit, blankets and books.

We need this gun now, my mother said. Eli says we need it because the police were here. Don't touch it ever. I'll teach you how to use it. On the weekend we'll go down to the river and practice, okay? We'll go early when there's no one around.

She handed me the pistol. It was small and black.

See, it's not heavy, she said. Eli says it has fifteen rounds. I can shoot it fifteen times before I have to put another magazine into it.

Where did he get this gun?

I don't know.

My mother said we would keep Eli's gun under the driver's seat, which was exactly where I kept all the objects I found in the dump. If anyone placed their hand under that seat they'd find a bag of mercury beads, marbles, one gold hoop earring, four brass buttons, and a gun.

The following Sunday we woke up early and went down to the river.

I'm not even scared of an alligator now that I have this gun in my hand, my mother said.

Do you really know how to use it?

Eli's been giving me lessons while you've been at school, she said. I'm a natural. A real natural. That's what Eli said. I think it's all my piano practice. I hit all the targets. It was easy. I got lucky every time. Eli said, when anyone shoots a gun, you don't have to do a whole lot to make it happen.

At the river, near the dock, my mother placed a white piece of paper on a tree. She'd drawn a black circle in the middle with a marker.

Eli made me do it blindfolded and I did, my mother said. I hit the mark every time.

At the river my mother repeated the words Eli had used to teach her. Use your dominant eye, she said. Do not squat, blink, or duck your head.

I stood square to the target and placed the gun up to my eye level.

You want something good to happen with that bullet, my mother said. That's what Eli said. You want something good to happen.

I didn't hit the target.

It's your little hand, my mother said. You really need a tiny child's gun.

My fifteen bullets only left holes in the air.

Do we really need to have this? I asked.

Eli gave me the gun, my mother said. It's a present.

Why?

Don't tell any of your friends we have it. Don't tell. It's to be safe. Protection.

Protection?

It's like an umbrella in the rain.

Why did Eli give it to you?

He thinks this pistol is like giving me roses, my mother said.

Eli thought that two girls living all alone in a car is all a gun needs.

natural *Naturtalent*

blindfolded *mit verbundenen Augen*

to squat *hinhocken*
to blink closing and opening your eyes quickly
to duck *den Kopf einziehen*
to stand square to stand directly facing sth.

13

After the police had threatened my mother and Eli had given us the gun, I had my first, last and only fight with April May. It was the only fight because we never made up and I lost her forever. I couldn't think of a dare or a trick or a bet to get her back. The words to make her forgive me didn't exist.

We'd always been friends. Her family was the only family who had been at the trailer park ever since the day my mother moved into our car in the visitors' parking area. Sergeant Bob told me my mother arrived dressed in her school uniform with a school bag filled with schoolbooks over her shoulder and a newborn in her arms. April May was practically a sister. And the worst thing was we had a fight about something we didn't even believe in or know about.

When I got to the dock by the river, April May was already there. I was in a good mood because I had cigarettes with me that I'd stolen from the Mexicans. Corazón and Ray had left some Marlboros on a chair and I managed to slip two out of the box.

April May was sitting cross-legged on the dock, much too close to the water.

Hey, move back a bit, I said as I gave her a cigarette. An alligator can pluck you out in a second.

April May shrugged and lit up.

I sat beside her and lit up my cigarette too.

Well, I said, if you're going to get attacked they can attack me too. The river can have us both.

Mouse Lick sb. who licks as gently as a mouse

You're a real friend, Mouse Lick, April May said.

Mouse Lick, seriously? Is that what you call me?

Well, yes.

That's my nickname?

Yes, Don't feel bad, April May said. It's not bad. Lick my cheek, come on. Do it.

No, I'm not licking your cheek. I can't believe this. You've been calling me Mouse Lick behind my back?

We were laughing and full of tobacco-smoke-filled smiles about this and then everything went wrong.

So, those cops didn't come back, right? April May said.

No. My mother thinks we might need to find other places to park our car for a while.

Maybe that's a good idea.

Yes, maybe. If we move, though, we'll need to stay near school and near my mother's job.

You know, April May said. I should tell you something, Pearl. Margot has not been going to work at all. She's going to lose that job. My dad told me today that your mother shouldn't be with Eli. My dad says Eli's not walking on God's good side.

That's not true, I said, and defended a man who'd broken into our lives and stolen my mother away from me.

My father says Eli's eating up your mother's sweet soul, April May said. He says Eli and Pastor Rex are gunrunning and that this buying guns for God is one big con.

No, Eli's a good man. Why did your dad say that?

My dad knows people, knows them inside-out. He was in the war. Eli's bad for your mother. What are you going to live on if your mother's not working?

My mother says your daddy is KKK, I said as if this were a tit-for-tat talk.

And I never should have said that, even if it were true.

April May closed her mouth. She threw her cigarette butt into the river. I knew it was sinking down to the river bed that was paved with bullets and where Pastor Rex's Jesus-on-the-cross toothbrush lay buried in the brown muck, mud, and dregs of gunpowder.

Your mother says my father is KKK? April May answered. Oh, really? Like a wizard or what?

I knew I should've kept my mouth shut. I wanted to grab the words out of the air and stuff them back into my mouth.

It's not true, April May said. Your mother's mistaken. I'm going to ask my father right away.

No, she's not mistaken, I answered. How do you know he isn't? Is there a black person living here? I don't see one. Your father's always controlling who comes and goes around here. My mother says your parents are racists and we're only friends with all of you because we have no other choice.

I couldn't stop myself even though I knew I should. My words flowed out of me in the stream of my breath and blew over the river, over palm trees, into the clouds and toward the ocean. I could not get them back.

The letter *k* was not just another letter. It should have been cut out of the alphabet with a knife.

gunrunning the activity of smuggling guns into a country
con (*infml.*) short for confidence; here: a trick based on abusing people's trust
to know sb. inside-out (*infml.*) to know everything about sb.

tit-for-tat *Wie du mir, so ich dir*

muck dirt
dregs *Bodensatz*

wizard Grand Wizard; title given to the head of the Ku Klux Klan

14

My mother soon forgot about the threats from the police and stopped talking about moving the car elsewhere. She was with Eli all the time.

I had nowhere else to go but the abandoned trailer.

Most days I went straight from school to the trailer and did my homework or read a book. Sometimes I just lay on the bottom bunk bed and smoked a cigarette from my Eli cigarette supply.

It didn't take me long to realize that someone else was using the trailer in the mornings while I was at school. At first I'd find a new cigarette butt in the sink, or some Kleenex rolled up in a ball under a window, or a newspaper lying on the bunk bed.

Once there was even someone's light-yellow urine in the toilet bowl.

And then the guns began to appear. At first there were two shotguns lying across the lower bunk.

Over the next days, the top bunk was filled to the ceiling with shotguns, machine guns, and pistols and then the bottom bunk was filled up too. In no time the weapons became stacks of metal rising in layers on both beds. After two weeks, the number of guns had grown to such a degree that the person keeping them had begun to divide them into types. The top bed was assigned to machine guns and the bottom bunk to rifles. Pistols and other handguns were now placed in two large boxes that took up most of the space between the bedroom area of the trailer and the kitchen.

stack a pile of things arranged on top of one another
layer *Lage, Schicht*

Now I could not lie on the bed and do my homework and so I sat in the kitchen at the kitchen counter filling in my copybooks and doing my reading assignments. I stopped working every now and again to look over at the collection of weapons.

From this side of the trailer, I could also look out the window at the abandoned recreational area with the old swing set and slide.

One day I was so sleepy I just put my head down on the kitchen counter. In my half-awake dream, I heard the guns speak.

The guns told me about a seven-year-old girl and twenty-two-year old man shot in a drive-by shooting, two teenage boys fired at by cops, a two-year-old boy shot in a gang-related shootout in a park, twenty schoolchildren killed on a school bus, a mother dead in a supermarket, two women shot to death in a parking lot, twenty teenagers gunned down at the movies, a ten-year-old girl shot at a library, five college students slain at a football game, nine people shot at a church prayer meeting, a mother and a daughter shot in a car, four nuns gunned down at a bus stop, eight eight-year-old girls shot at a ballet class, two policemen shot in

to slay (slew, slain) (*old use, lit.*) to kill sb. in a violent way

their car, and a nine-year-old girl shot in a playground and shot at again and again, bullets breaking trees to shreds, ninety holes in the sky from a machine gun, gunshots in a rainstorm killing raindrops, twenty bullets for the moon, words broken by gunfire, words pierced by bullets so the alphabet became a b c l r s t x z, lovers fallen, tears and bullets on the floor, my dearest, my-one-and-only, my little one, one-of-a-kind, we are all one-of-a-kind, and all lonely and all afraid and all looking for love bullets everywhere.

Then, as a part of the gun-song dream, I heard a person walk slowly up the stairs to the trailer.

I lifted my head and watched as the door handle moved downward. There was fumbling. Somcthing fell and was picked up. A kick pushed the door open.

Corazón walked into the trailer. She carried six shotguns cradled in her arms. She turned toward the pile of guns and laid them down in the rifle pile on the bottom of the bunk bed.

Then she turned to leave and, as she walked toward the door, she saw me.

Ay, bebe, she said, and pressed her hand against her heart. You scared me. You so quiet.

Corazón?

Sí, bebé. ¿Qué haces aqui? What are you doing here?

She walked toward me and could see the pages of my schoolwork spread out on the kitchen counter.

Why you here? she asked.

I'm doing my homework.

She nodded. She knew. Everyone knew that my mother and Eli were a sweetheart thing.

Corazón stepped closer to me. She smiled and her big brown eyes grew small. She held out her hand to me.

Come on. You cannot be here. Ay, bebe, she said. You do your work in my house, yes?

She touched the top of my head and wove her fingers into my hair. Your hair is soft, she said. So white, like flour.

Corazón caressed the top of my head, smoothing down my frizzy light yellow-white hair.

You're not staying here, she said and picked me up. I was so small and skinny everyone always wanted to pick me up as if I were a six-year-old.

We're going to my house now, Corazón said. She's waiting for you and I have some M&M's.

Corazón's English was good, but she could never understand that objects in English did not have a gender and so she turned everything into a she or a he.

to pierce to make holes through sth. with a sharp object

to cradle sth. to hold sth. gently, esp. by supporting with the arms

to caress [kə'res] to touch or kiss sb. in a gentle or loving way
frizzy very curly and not smooth or shiny

laundry detergent *Waschmittel*
Joy, Dove, Ajax, Lysol ['laɪsɒl] brand names of cleaning or disinfecting products

to squeeze sb. tight *jdn. fest an sich drücken*

I wrapped my legs around her waist and my arms around her neck. While she held my with one hand against her, she picked up my school workbook and tucked it under her arm. Corazón smelled like Joy lemon dishwashing liquid, Dove soap, Tide laundry detergent, Ajax, and Lysol. I could be standing in the cleaning-products aisle of the supermarket.

Never come back here, promise, she said. This trailer, he's for keeping the guns.

Corazón carried me out and past the swing set and slide. She walked me around Pastor Rex's and Mrs. Roberta Young's trailers and toward her own.

Corazón squeezed me tight as she carried me past the plastic gremlin and five plastic pink flamingos and toward her trailer. I liked being her baby.

Never go back to that place again, Corazón said.

I looked over her shoulder back at Noelle's field of dolls. Bees hovered in small clouds in search of pollen in their red and yellow doll hair.

15

I no longer spent my afternoons and evenings in the abandoned trailer, and went to visit Corazón instead.

The Mexicans had guns everywhere too.

There were shotguns lined up against one wall and in stacks in the hallway leading to the bedrooms. In both bedrooms machine guns were kept under the beds. The living room had large bins filled with pistols. There were also boxes of ammunition piled high along the walls of almost every room.

We would sit at the kitchen counter. While Corazón cleaned the used guns, I usually did my homework. Sometimes we'd talk or listen to music.

She also let me watch Mexican soap operas on television.

Mexican telenovelas are better than life, Corazón said. Somebody will study this one day and know it's true.

She gave me Sprite to drink and served me potato chips, Mars bars, doughnuts, and M&M's. She also made bags of popcorn in her microwave. She and Ray ate only junk food.

Corazón dismantled the firearms and then used a rag to remove the thick, caked-on carbon buildup. She also wiped off any old oil and powder buildup that had not burned. The white-and-red rags turned black as she worked. Then she'd apply a solvent, which she'd let sit for a couple of minutes. Often she had to scrub the whole gun with a toothbrush to get inside the cracks. Then she'd wipe the gun clean with a lint-free cloth. Sometimes she used a bore brush to break up any buildup inside the barrel, and she used oil on the areas that rotate in the trigger or added grease to the sliding parts. She had full and empty syringes of Lubriplate lying about on the countertops of the kitchen and in the living-room area.

After cleaning the guns, Corazón had to attach a label on each weapon as identification. She wrote it out in black marker on a yellow label tag with string that she looped around the grip frame. She had several Brownells catalogs, which she used for looking up to find the kind of gun she was tagging. Corazón let me help her do this, as she thought my handwriting was better than hers. This was how I learned about firearms.

Pastor Rex and Eli owned the weapons. They got them from Pastor Rex's gun program, bought them from the veterans at the hospital, or purchased them at gun shows.

Corazón cleaned them and Ray helped Eli resell them in Texas, but mostly he took them across the border and into Mexico.

telenovela a television soap opera

to dismantle to take a machine apart into pieces
rag *Lappen*
caked-on *verkrustet*
carbon buildup *Kohlerückstände*
solvent *Lösungsmittel*
to let sth. sit *etw. einwirken lassen*

lint-free *flusenfrei*
bore brush *Laufreinigungsbürste*
barrel *Gewehrrohr*
to rotate to turn like a wheel
trigger *Abzug*
grease fat or oil
syringe [sɪˈrɪndʒ] *Spritze*
Lubriplate brand name of a machine oil

grip frame the metal handle of a gun
Brownells US company that sells firearms and ammunition

Corazón smoked the whole time. She even had an old-fashioned stand-up ashtray that was piled high with yellow filters stuck in fine beach sand.

She was so nice, one afternoon I dared to ask her if I could smoke too, and she laughed and handed me a cigarette.

As the afternoon drew into dusk, the trailer filled with smoke. Corazón said that the first thing she did when she moved into the trailer was to deactivate the stupid gringo smoke alarm.

gringo (*infml., disapproving*) used in Latin American countries to refer to people from the US

When Corazón was not working on the guns, she washed her trailer. I'd never been in such a spotless place before. No wonder she smelled like cleaning liquids and soaps. It was her reaction to living so close to a garbage dump.

On one wall, Corazón had a large poster of the singer Selena Quintanilla dressed in a purple jumpsuit. Above the photograph were the words: *Selena Queen of Tejano Music.* Underneath the poster was a plaster figure of the Virgin of Guadalupe.

jumpsuit *Overall*
Tejano music Texan-Mexican music; folk music
plaster *Gips*

Those are the two women I love, Corazón said.

She listened to Selena all the time and her dream was to visit Selena's grave.

She's buried in Corpus Christi and that means the body of Christ, Corazón said. That's where she is in Texas, Corpus Christi, Texas.

Corpus Christi a coastal city in the south of Texas

Thanks to Corazón I began to memorize Selena's songs. She told me Selena was killed when she was only twenty-three years old and had been shot to death by her manager.

The song I liked best was 'Si una vez,' and used to sing it while I did my homework and Corazón was cleaning the guns. It only took her a few days of hearing me sing along to realize I could sing. I told her my mother had raised me on love songs.

si una vez 'If I once'; a song by Selena published in 1994; in which she questions why she fell in love with an abusive partner

Corazón put down the rifle she was cleaning. She walked over to the CD player and turned it off.

Sing it again, Pearlita, she said. Sing it.

In the quiet trailer I sang the song and Corazón said, You're like the reincarnation of Selena. How can you sing like a Tejana? How can you sing like a Mexican?

I knew she was exaggerating. Corazón exaggerated everything as if words could change things.

I'm going to teach you all about Selena, she said. It was a .38-caliber Taurus revolver that was used to kill her. You know the one, the small one I was cleaning yesterday? Just like that one. I thought that if anyone walked toward the trailer on one of those days, they would have seen smoke curling out of the windows and heard someone singing inside.

Ray never said a word to me. Corazón said he was a quiet man and that talking to people was never going to happen. And he never asked what I was doing there. Corazón explained to me that

Mexicans will never allow people to be alone. She said, We even have a proverb about this. We always say it is better to be poor than live alone.

Every evening when Ray came home from work, he walked into the smoke cloud, lit a cigarette, and joined the bonfire.

bonfire *Freudenfeuer*

16

hairdo (*old-fashioned*) hairstyle

After we had cleaned and labeled the guns, Corazón liked to dress me up and make up my face and my fingernails. She also liked to make elaborate hairdos using hairpieces she'd buy at Walmart.

pail *Scheuereimer*
mop *Scheuerlappen*

My mother never asked what I was doing while she was in the car with Eli. I never told her April May and I had a fight. And Rose never told my mother she never saw me anymore because, after the two policemen came to investigate our car, my mother stopped working at the hospital and never went back. Her pails and mops were left behind, along with her last paycheck.

My mother explained she'd left her work at the hospital because she couldn't stand to be near so many wounded men.

They keep coming, she said. It will never end, not until the end of the world. Why bother to work or go to school? Maybe you should stay home from school now. What's the point?

One day as I walked back to the car, after having been with Corazón, I saw my mother standing outside the Mercury in her lavender nightgown. She was by the back of the car with the trunk open. She was with a man I'd never seen. His car was parked side by side next to ours.

My mother held a long green felt cloth in her hand. She was pulling a silver fork and spoon out of one felt pocket in the cloth and holding it out for the man to look at. She was selling our silverware.

My mother was selling our belongings.

wad *Bündel*

Almost every day someone turned up at the trailer park to sell guns to Pastor Rex and Eli. As the people left with a wad of gun cash in their pocket, my mother would stop them and offer something for almost nothing out of our trunk.

I couldn't stop her.

Kotex brand name of feminine hygiene products

For the Limoges she bought a box of Cheerios, a jar of peanut butter and a can of Raid. The antique music box was worth two boxes of Kotex and a can of powdered milk. For the violin she bought a box of aspirin and some toothpaste.

She sold every piece of silverware for a quarter apiece.

a steal *ein Schnäppchen*
on a regular basis regularly

It's a steal, I heard her say to a man who came to sell guns to Pastor Rex on a regular basis.

He was a tall, skinny man with deeply red, sunburned skin. He always wore jeans that were too large. The denims were kept on his hips by a belt with a huge belt buckle that had a hole in the center, which was a beer-bottle opener.

Savage Arms a US gunmaker

Woman, he said, listen to me. I've just sold a rifle that killed a bear. Why would I want to buy a spoon when I've just sold a Savage?

Well, to help me out, I guess, my mother answered.

Within a few weeks everything was gone.

I knew the next stop would be to stand with my mother at a red light with my hand held out, begging at car windows.

On the night she sold the last Limoges plate we lay in the dark in silence. Outside, as on several nights a month, we could hear the sound of gunfire in the distance. On this night the sound seemed closer.

Someone is shooting, I said. Are you awake? Do you hear it?

Yes, my mother answered. Some man is down at the river shooting at the sky. He's shooting angels.

17

The following Friday afternoon the piano arrived.

From Corazón's trailer kitchen window I saw the truck drive past the dump and move down the highway toward town and the church. There was a black piano painted on the side of the truck. This was Pastor Rex's dream come true. He said that singing hymns to a DVD player plugged into a wall behind the altar was a sacrilege. He truly believed that most people went to church because of the music.

sacrilege ['sækrɪlɪdʒ] the act of treating sth. holy without respect

Music is what elevates us to God, he said.

to elevate to raise in mind and feelings

Pastor Rex managed to convince everyone to donate money and organize fund-raisers to get the piano and it had taken him over a year to accomplish his mission. He was able finally to buy an old piano from the 1950s.

to accomplish sth. to finish sth. successfully

This is God's present to us all, he said.

No one at church knew how to play the piano except for Pastor Rex, and so he agreed both to play and to give the service.

The Friday the piano arrived was also the day a great thunderstorm broke over us.

From the kitchen window Corazón and I watched the downpour. We could see Mrs. Roberta Young's trailer and Noelle's field of dolls.

The storm lasted twenty minutes. Rain fell in large drops and then the drops became stones of ice. When the rain stopped, everything was white.

Corazón and I went outside. The air was damp and clean as if everything had been washed. The Barbie dolls were buried under piles of hailstones.

Look over there. Look at the dump, Corazón said.

The dump had become a white mountain.

Everyone went to church that Sunday to see the piano. Even Corazón and Ray and my mother made an exception and went to a Protestant church just to see and hear the instrument.

My mother wore white wrist-length gloves she'd found in an old plastic bag that also contained stockings she'd never worn.

stockings *Seidenstrümpfe*

It's a disgrace the women don't wear gloves to church, she said.

disgrace *Schande*

That Sunday the church was packed. I'd never seen so many people in attendance. Everyone had come to hear the piano.

in attendance present

From our pew I could see April May and her parents. It was the first time I'd seen her outside of school since our fight. She'd obviously told Sergeant Bob and Rose that my mother thought he was Ku Klux Klan, as they didn't walk over and approach us as they would normally have done.

In another pew right at the front Noelle and Mrs. Roberta Young were sitting beside Corazón and Ray. For this occasion, Corazón had fixed her long, curly hair in a round bun at the top of her head. She had a perfect pin curl in the middle of her forehead. She'd also wrapped a pink ribbon around the bun and tied it in a bow. It was a true Selena look.

Eli walked into the church with Pastor Rex. Everyone I knew in the world was gathered together for the first time in one place. I took my mother's hand and realized it had been a long time since we'd held hands.

When my mother saw Eli come she said, Oh, he's here, he's here. He came. Oh, this is good.

Eli walked over toward us and slipped in next to my mother so that he sat between us. She placed her hand on his thigh and it was as if she was holding on to a banister or rail. It seemed to make her steady. When she heard the wounded vets being brought into the back of the church, she closed her eyes and fell asleep to the anthem of crutches and wheelchairs.

Eli leaned forward and whispered to me, Is she all right?

Sleepy, I said. She's going to play the piano. Did she tell you?

Eli reached for the pack of cigarettes in the front pocket of his shirt. He knocked the pack against his wrist until a few were loosened out. He gave one to me. Eli gave me a cigarette because he knew I was for sale. He knew how much I cost. It only took one to keep me happy.

I slipped the Camel up my sleeve.

At the pulpit, before the service began, Pastor Rex announced that this church service was named Praise for the Piano Worship. We have our piano now, he said. We're truly blessed.

Everyone in the church clapped.

During the course of the service, Pastor Rex had to move from the pulpit over to the piano to play the hymns. At first everyone was quiet and leaned way forward to hear the music but Pastor Rex didn't play well and made many mistakes. He had to slow down in the middle of a hymn and draw up close to the sheet music to try and figure out what the notes were. No one could sing along. The initial excitement had turned into a quiet discomfort. The church had become a theater, and Pastor Rex's failure was the act.

At the end of the service, my mother and I stayed seated as the congregation slowly filed out of the building. Even Pastor Rex left the church to go outside to say goodbye to everyone.

The day before, my mother had promised to play for me, but was worried. She'd not touched a piano for so many years.

Eli stood up.

Don't you want to hear my mother play? I asked Eli.

bun *Knoten*

pin curl a curl made usually by dampening a strand of hair with water or lotion, coiling it and securing it with a hairpin or clip

banister handrail; *Geländer*
rail *Geländer*

anthem here: a religious song sung by a choir with organ music

discomfort a feeling of uneasiness

to file out to march out

Mary had a Little Lamb a 19th century nursing rhyme
Three Blind Mice a 17th century nursing rhyme
to illuminate to light sth. up
key *Taste*
starred *sternenbesetzt*
constellation normally, a groups of stars; here: the whole set-up
Rachmaninoff's Concerto No. 2, in C Minor, Opus 18 a concerto for piano and orchestra composed in 1900, one of Rachmaninoff's most popular pieces
minor *in Moll*
to die here: to sink

I'm sure it's sweeter than sweet, he said. I'll hear her another time. I need to tell Ray about something.
Eli turned and walked toward the door.
I'm sure he thought my mother was going to play 'Mary had a Little Lamb' or 'Three Blind Mice.'
Pastor Rex also left the church following quickly behind Eli.
My mother didn't look over her shoulder. She just closed her eyes and, after a few minutes, asked, Has everyone gone?
Almost everyone, I said.
We stood and walked up the aisle to the piano.
As she was so small, my mother first pushed the piano bench close to the instrument so that she could reach the foot pedals.
Once she had everything in place, she slowly peeled off the gloves and gave them to me to hold. I stuffed them in the pocket of my dress.
My mother sat at the piano. The small spotlight that hung above the altar illuminated her yellow hair. She placed her fingers on the black and white keys. Her hands were starred with tiny freckles and her nails were painted with Moon-Blue nail polish. The blue opal ring that her piano teacher had given to her was part of the constellation.
My mother raised her hands and slowly brought them down to the piano. She played the first chord.
Those who had not yet left the building stood still. A few wounded soldiers, who were still sitting in the back, closed their eyes.
April May, who was almost out the front door, stopped to listen.
Those who were not too far outside the church and heard a few notes walked back in and stood in silence.
One music chord can make the world stop.
My mother played Rachmaninoff's Piano Concerto No. 2 in C Minor, Opus 18. I'd heard it on the radio a few times and she hummed it many times as she played the music on the car's dashboard.
In the church my mother's small hands opened and her fingers reached and found full octaves.
My mother bowed her head and the music came out of her. Her hands were flying, falling, and dying as they moved across the instrument.
As my mother played, the gloom and beauty of Russia fell like a darkness over the state of Florida and turned the Sunshine State into the saddest place on Earth.

18

Monday morning, the day after my mother played the piano at church, we talked in the car for a while before getting up.

Inside the Mercury, the sound of crickets and birds mixed with the sound of trucks and cars moving down the highway.

My mother said, I always used to protect my hands. I'd forgotten. I used to avoid hammers and nails and opening jars. I was fearful of getting my fingers caught in a door or being cut by a knife in the kitchen.

Do you think we can go back to the church later today, after school? I asked. I want to hear you play the piano again.

Now I use my hands as if they had no value, my mother said.

We'll go to the church in the afternoon. When I get back from school.

Yes, before nightfall.

But nightfall never came because the day never had a night. The sun never stopped burning that day up.

It was Noelle who told me what had happened.

Noelle had stepped out for a moment to hang some clothes on the short laundry line tied between a tree and her trailer.

She'd heard and seen it all.

The truth is you never know when it's your last day, Noelle said. You never know.

She told me that, after I'd left for school my mother had stepped out of the Mercury and walked out of the visitors' parking area, through the main gate, and into the trailer park.

A young man had been sitting on the cracked plastic swing in the recreation area gently rocking back and forth. He had curly hair, blue eyes, and was wearing a thick black wool sweater. He had a gun in his right hand. Eli was standing beside the man and they were talking. Noelle could not hear what they were saying.

As my mother walked barefoot toward the park's bathroom, the young man pulled himself out of the swing and moved toward her in a few quick strides.

Noelle said that Eli called out my mother's name.

My mother stopped walking when she saw the gun in the young man's hand.

Noelle said the young man and my mother had moved close enough for her to overhear everything that was said.

Lady, why are you wearing a nightgown? the young man asked.

I just woke up.

You run around in your pajamas?

I live here, my mother said.

Why aren't you wearing shoes?

curly not straight; *lockig*

stride a long step

pajamas (*US*) pyjamas

It's warm.
Then he held up the gun and pointed it at my mother.
You're going to shoot me, she said.
Yes.
I understand this is what's going to happen, my mother said.
Yes, he answered. Now I declare new things.

caring *Kulturbeutel*

I knew my mother's caring was set on fire when he started to shoot.
My mother knew he had hitchhiked across the United States, from California to Florida, in order to see if love existed in America.

BB gun a type of gun which fires small metal balls using air pressure

Inside his body my mother could see electric trains, toy trucks, Halloween candy, and toy guns, and even a BB gun for killing birds.
She felt the sunburn on his shoulders.
My mother knew all this young man needed was love. He needed a girl to take his hand and pull him into her bed.
Love did not exist in America.
My mother walked straight into the shooting gun like she was walking into a water sprinkler on a hot Florida day in July: wet me wet me shoot me shoot me wet me shoot me.

Part Two

19

Mr. Don't Come Back came back.

As I heard the story, I knew exactly what my mother had been thinking the moment she was shot. What Rose called my mother's empathy malady was my inheritance. It was passed on to me like her fear of a gas leak from a kitchen oven.

I heard everything from Noelle when she came to pick me up at school. I'd never seen her outside of the trailer park before except at church.

On the day of my mother's death, as I left the school building, Noelle walked toward me in her stiff, tiptoe Barbie-doll walk.

One cannot walk home alone, Noelle said.

Why?

Silence is also a judgment, she said. A rabbit can be afraid of the moon. Death visits every house.

Just tell me, please. Just be clear.

A kid with a gun killed your mama. I heard everything. I saw everything.

At first I was quiet.

Did you hear me, Noelle said. Margot was shot. A kid with a gun killed your mama. Pearl, she's dead.

At first I was quiet. And then I was so grateful that my heart beat by itself because I knew I would never be able to make it work if I had to do it. My heart's independent beats, beats that worked no matter what terrible thing had happened, made me feel tenderness toward my body and my insignificant life.

As we walked along the highway toward the trailer park, Noelle reached out and took my hand. I was fourteen years old, but did not have to count how many people had held my hand before this moment. I didn't need math. Noelle's hand in mine felt so large compared to my mother's child-sized hand.

Many times my mother had said she hoped I would die before she did.

You won't be able to survive life without me, my mother explained. It will hurt so bad. There isn't even a song for it yet. Pearl, I hope you die first.

My mother was right, I should have died first.

Eli's down at the police station, Noelle said.

What's Eli got to do with this?

Nothing. Well, he sold the kid the gun and he was there when it all happened. Well, he didn't really sell it. It was a trade. That kid

malady illness
inheritance *Nachlass, Erbe*

beat *Herzschlag*
tenderness kind and sympathetic feeling

gave Eli his silver belt as a trade for the gun. And Eli was even wearing the belt when the cops took him away. It was fancy. It was silver with a gold eagle engraved in the center.

After Mr. Don't Come Back left us, my mother had missed him. She felt the absence of her destiny.

to turn one's pockets inside out (*infml.*) to reveal all one has

And wherever Eli was, he was holding his head high as if he'd stolen everyone's good fortune. He was never, ever going to turn his pockets inside out. I knew the song.

I'm sorry, Noelle said. I wish I'd been your friend and now it's too late. Who knows where you're going to live now. It's afterward when we wish we'd been kind. I wish I'd baked you a cake and taken it to your car and let you use our bathroom to shower. I didn't think of these things. I should have given you some of my dolls. I didn't really know that you and Margot mattered.

I stayed quiet. I listened to my heart. It beat as if every day were the same day.

I'm sorry, Noelle said again. I saw everything. Your mother tried to stop those bullets with her hands.

I looked over at Noelle. In the opening of her blouse, in the pocket place between her breasts, lay a dead swallow.

form *Formular*

There was a young woman dressed in a blue suit from Child Protective Service sitting inside the Mercury waiting for me. She was on the passenger side with the door wide open, filling in some forms on her lap. She didn't even know she was sitting in my bedroom.

As Noelle and I approached, the woman got out of the car.

She said, You must be Pearl.

I nodded.

I still couldn't speak. It was as if a superstition had taken over me, which I didn't even know I had. I thought, if I speak, all this will be true. I knew the words spoken would turn into the truth lived.

The trailer park was very quiet.

to witness sth. to see sth. happen, esp. an accident or crime

Most everyone is at the police station giving formal statements as to what they saw or heard, Noelle said. They already talked to me because I was the only person who witnessed it all. Life can surprise you.

And Eli? Well, he's not even considered a witness, Noelle said, as if she knew what I'd been thinking. He's part of the story. He got the child the gun. What were they doing there hanging out at the swing anyway?

to chew on sth. here: to think about

I wasn't speaking but I was placing Eli's name in my pocket like something I was going to chew on later.

duffel bag *Seesack*

The woman from Child Protective Services walked over to her car, which was parked right behind the Mercury, and took out a large and empty army-green duffel bag from the backseat.

Go to your car, girl, and pack up your stuff, she said.

She opened her trunk.

Put your things in here, she ordered, and got back into her own car behind the wheel.

Noelle said, I'll help you.

I still did not hear any word come out of me.

Noelle held open the duffel bag while I put in my bags of clothes, dolls, and books and all of my mother's plastic supermarket bags filled with her things.

I also ripped off my drawing of the solar system that we'd stuck on the back of the driver's seat and put that in too.

Since my mother always said I was smart, I reached under the driver's seat and took out the small black gun Eli had given to us.

I didn't look at Noelle, but I knew she'd seen the weapon because she said, Hey, Pearl, careful with that. You'd better not take that.

Noelle had known me all my life, but she didn't seem to know that 'you'd better not' were my three favorite words.

I pushed Eli's gun down deep into the duffel bag and then added in my collection of things I'd found in the dump.

After taking everything out of the car, there was only one thing left for me to get. I pulled the lever that opened the trunk and walked around and looked inside. All the trunk treasures were gone. I looked at the empty space that had once held silverware, Limoges plates, crystal wineglasses, a violin, a music box, the Chinese elephant-tusk boat, and my mother's silk bags of jewels.

The only thing left was the long silk box with a yellow ribbon. It didn't fit in the duffel bag, but I took it anyway.

I closed the trunk and walked around the car and made sure the windows were rolled up and closed the doors.

I left the key in the ignition. We'd never turned that key and driven somewhere. We'd been parked for almost fifteen years.

ignition *Zündung; Zündschloss*

Are you finished now? the woman called out as she rolled her window down. It's late. Let's go. Get in the car.

Noelle walked me to the passenger side and opened the door.

You know, Pearl, Noelle said. We all liked your mother even though she was never one of us. I think my mother said that about her once.

I nodded.

You will take a long, long trip, Noelle said, and handed me a piece of Trident gum. Here, take this, she said. It's all I have.

I put the gum in my mouth and got in the car and closed the door.

For a second I pressed my palm to the window's glass inside and Noelle did the same on the outside.

If April May had been with me she would have said, That Noelle is thinking about Eli, thinking she has a chance now that your mama's dead. By tomorrow she'll be baking him some cookies. By tomorrow she'll be spraying on perfume. She'll be his shoulder to cry on.

The woman from Child Protective Services turned the key, and the motor started up. The ice air from the air-conditioning blew into the car as the wintergreen gum filled my mouth with the taste of pinecones.

I like it very cold in here, so I hope you don't mind, the woman said.

She backed the car out of the visitors' parking area and away from the sign that said WELCOME TO INDIAN WATERS TRAILER PARK. Then she turned the steering wheel to the right and drove onto the highway.

to swivel to turn around and look in another direction

I thought about swiveling in my seat to look out the back window as we drove away, but I didn't. There was no one waving goodbye.

In the car the woman said, I tell this to all the kids that I pick up. Please don't be calling me every time you fall and scrape your knee or something. I'm your social worker. You're my case. No, no, I ain't a lost relative, some aunt or something or Mary Poppins. I'm taking you to your foster family. And listen, only call me if there's an emergency. Put on your seat belt.

ain't (*infml.*) am not
Mary Poppins a 1964 American fantasy musical film about Mary Poppins, a nanny who visits a dysfunctional family in London

I didn't answer. I clipped on my seat belt. I looked out the window. I chewed Noelle's gum.

So, you're wondering if you can see your mother. Every kid I pick up wants to do this because they don't believe in death so, listen to me clearly, that's never going to happen. Nobody's going to let you see her, girl. She's full of holes. No, I haven't seen her, not personally, no, but that's what I heard someone say. One of those cops said your mother's full of holes.

I didn't answer.

Why are you so quiet? Huh? You deaf? You're funny-looking and you don't talk? You don't even cry for your mama? I'm not seeing any wet tears on your face.

I didn't answer.

Well, if you're not going to talk, you can read then. Here's your file. Read it for yourself. Those papers will tell you everything you need to know.

file *Akte*

With one hand on the steering wheel, the woman swiveled and reached into the backseat and passed me a few pages that were stapled inside a yellow file. Then she drove me away from my car-home, the dump, the swing set, and the killed river.

to staple sth. *etw. zusammenheften, -tackern*

The CPS social worker turned on the radio and drove me away from my childhood.

If my mother had been in the backseat, driving with us, she'd have said, You think you get a dose of tragedy and that's that. You

dose a measured amount of sth., such as medicine

think it can't get worse and that you're saved now. But tragedy is not like medicine. You don't get a dose like a pill or spoonful. Tragedy always kicks in.

And this time it was not pretend. This time I was really driving away from the trailer park, down the highway in the direction of Sarasota. We took a left up at the first light, then a left, and then a right on the ramp and through the row of palm trees, past the Walmart. My eyes followed the long white line painted on the asphalt in the middle of the highway. That long white line was a river that led from Niagara Falls straight to the Gulf of Mexico.

My mother would have said, Drive fast. Let's get a speeding ticket. Leave skid marks.

My mind was a grammar book full of question marks. Who killed her? Why? How did it happen? Where was I going? Who cared about me? Would I see my mother? Where would I live? Would I ever see April May or Corazón again? Where was Eli? Would they find my mother's family? Where would I go to school? Whom did I belong to?

I opened the pages on my lap and read the section in my file that was a Xerox copy of the police report. It had been filed only a few minutes after I'd left for school. She'd been dead for seven hours. I'd lived for seven hours thinking I was in her thoughts.

I read every word in my file.

The first page contained a policeman's report: White woman in her late twenties shot twenty times at the entrance to Indian Waters Trailer Park. Attempted to get a pulse on the woman but none was found. No witnesses of the shooting came forward, but shots were heard at 8:15 a.m. Several residents said they heard at least twenty shots fired. Rose Smith and her husband Sergeant Bob Smith said that they didn't give it much importance because shots were always being heard in the area, as people like shooting at the river for alligators. Rose Smith said the victim was Margot France and that she was homeless living with her daughter, Pearl, in the Mercury parked outside the trailer park. Corazón Luz and her husband Ray Luz, also residents, both said they were not at home at the time. Pastor Rex Wood, also a resident, said he had not heard anything. The shooter was found dead on the ground next to the victim. His driver's license issued in California said his name was Paul Luke Mathews, sex male, race white, eyes blue. Height 6 ft. Mathews seems to have gone to the trailer park to sell his gun in an anti-violence, gun-buying program run by the local church. Mathews appears to have killed the victim, identified by the neighbors as Margot France, and then killed himself. The scene was secured with crime scene tape.

My mother was killed twenty times.

Sarasota a city in the southwest of Florida
ramp an artificial slope; *Rampe*

to issue sth. to hand sth. out for use

6 ft. (*abbr.*) *ca. 1.83m* (foot/feet; 1 foot equals 0.3048 metres)

As I read the report, Laura Nyro's voice singing 'Wedding Bell Blues' came through the car's speakers. It was one of my mother's favorite songs.

The second page of my file had only one sentence. It stated: Victim's only known relative is a daughter, Pearl France.

My life was nine words long.

I closed the file and looked out the window.

I took Noelle's chewing gum out of my mouth and reached under the car seat to stick it there. My fingers felt several hard, round bumps of other pieces left behind. This social worker's car seat was a graveyard of children's chewing gum.

The woman turned the music way up. She wanted to make sure the radio was too loud for a conversation. I'm sure she was sick and tired of talking to leftover kids.

Laura Nyro's voice filled up the car and no other sound fit inside.

As we drove away from the trailer park and away from the Mercury, away from April May and Noelle, it began to drizzle. I felt our puzzled land bow toward me. A break in the clouds lit up the inside of the car. I felt the trees lean, the highways rise, even the noonday Florida sun seemed to draw closer to my orbit.

orbit *Umlaufbahn; Dunstkreis*

As the raindrops spotted the car window I heard my mother's voice. She filled me up like a song. She said, When a little girl loses her mother, because her mother becomes a stranger's target practice, even the rain falls with grace.

grace *Anmut*

20

The foster home was a large two-story house surrounded by a garden in the suburbs of Sarasota.

As we approached the house, the social worker turned off the radio and explained that the house belonged to Mr. David Brodsky. He and his wife, who had died a few years ago, had fostered children for decades. Mr. Brodsky took in children who were in an emergency situation until a more permanent solution could be found.

The system's broken. Broken, the social worker said. Normally you wouldn't have kids staying with an old man, we like families, but there's no one taking in kids. What can you do? Beggars can't be choosers, right? Am I right?

She turned off the motor.

Mr. Brodsky takes in the shoots because they're the emergency cases. It's hard to find someone who can take you in fast. There're two other shoots staying here now. We call you children shoots because your parents were shot.

The social worker opened the car door and leaned forward and released the lever of the trunk.

Listen, she said. While you're here, in the meantime, Child Protective Services and the police will be looking around to see if you have any relatives they can call. They couldn't find anything in your car that linked you to a family. You sure you don't know of any kin? An aunt or cousin? Is there someone? There must be someone.

I shook my head.

I never can understand these families with just two people in them! How can a family get so small? And where's your father anyway? My files are full of mother-and-child families. Two people!

I didn't answer. I knew my schoolteacher father was somewhere carrying his other children on his shoulders and I didn't even know his name.

Someday you're going to have to remember how to talk, she said. And come on, open the door, hurry up. Get out of the car. Move it. Hurry. I've got four other kids I need to deal with today.

As the warm air from the garden encircled my body, I was so grateful to get out of the North Pole-cold car. My mother was dead and yet I could still feel gratitude for something.

The social worker reached into the trunk and took out the duffel bag and dropped it on the ground. She'd done this dozens of times.

suburb an area on the edge of a large town; *Vorstadt*

beggars can't be choosers (*saying*) *In der Not frisst der Teufel Fliegen; In der Not schmeckt jedes Brot*

kin (*old-fashioned*) family or relations

gratitude *Dankbarkeit*

What's this box? she asked as she took it out and laid it on top of the bag. It looks fancy.

narrow-rimmed glasses with a thin rim

Mr. Brodsky came out of the house to greet us. He was tall and slim. He had thick, curly hair and wore a pair of black narrow-rimmed round glasses.

It's good to see you, he said.

Listen, this shoot's not talking, the social worker said. Good luck getting a word out.

Laundromat *Waschsalon*

Dropping off a child was as routine to her as dumping the laundry at a Laundromat. I knew I was just a sack of something.

I've got to run, she said, and headed back to the car.

I was surprised to find I didn't want her to leave. During the drive, it was as if she'd become the only person I knew.

Mr. Brodsky got down on his knees so that he could look at me face-to-face.

I could hear the social worker start her car and drive off behind me. She was the link to my trailer park, the bridge between this foster home and my car. She was the last person who knew I belonged to something.

Mr. Brodsky said, I've known every kind of child. Your name is Pearl and that's a nice name. I think I've had a child with every name of the alphabet in this house. I hope you're a gentle person. I am. I know why you're here. I'm so sorry. Really, I am so, so sorry.

Now I knew people would be saying they were sorry to me forever after. I knew right then I'd be running away from the word 'sorry' for the rest of my life.

to tuck sth. under one's arm *unter den Arm klemmen*

Mr. Brodsky tucked the long box under his arm and picked up the duffel bag. He was strong and lifted the bundle with ease.

Let's go inside, he said. I'll show you your room.

I walked behind him into the house.

You also need to know there are two other children who live here. Helen, who's eight years old, and Leo, who's seventeen. They're both at school now. You won't be going to school, Mr. Brodsky continued. You're only going to be here for a few weeks while they find a more permanent home, so there's no point.

to frame sth. *etw. einrahmen*
lace *Spitze*
chest of drawers *Kommode mit Schubladen*
bedspread *Tagesdecke*
rug *Teppich*
closet *Wandschrank*
hanger *Kleiderbügel*

The bedroom had a high ceiling and the walls were painted white. There was a large window framed by white lace curtains, which looked down on the front garden and playhouse. The room contained a chest of drawers, a bed covered in a white bedspread, and a desk and chair. There was a round dark-blue rug on the floor. There was also a closet. The door was open and it was empty inside except for a row of pink satin-lined hangers. On the wall there was a painting of a night sky with stars.

The room smelled like fresh paint. Everything was so fresh and clean, it seemed that no one could ever have lived in the room before.

I knew the first thing I'd do as soon as Mr. Brodsky left was to lie down on the bed. When you grow up in a car, you dream about lying on sheets. I was also going to hunt down the shower.

to hunt down to look for, search

Mr. Brodsky placed the box and the duffel bag on the bed covered with a white lace bedspread.

What's the pretty box about? he asked.

I walked over from the doorway and placed my hand on the silk box. I looked into Mr. Brodsky's kind face.

I knew these were going to be the first words I was going to speak here in my new life.

Long gone, I said. Long gone.

Mr. Brodsky didn't answer. There was no way he could know my mother was in me singing 'Long Gone Blues' as if it were her funeral march.

It's a wedding dress, I said. My grandmother's wedding dress.

Oh, I see, Mr. Brodsky said.

My mother always dreamed she'd wear it one day, I said. It was a dream. And she also had a dream that I would wear it.

Mr. Brodsky was quiet for a few seconds as he looked down at the box that lay between us.

I breathed in deeply. It seemed to be the first breath I'd taken since Noelle picked me up at school a few hours ago.

Well, sometimes a dream is better than life, Mr. Brodsky said.

Yes.

No. she won't ever wear it, but she had the dream that she wore it.

Yes, I said.

When Mr. Brodsky said a dream was better than life, I knew he was one of us. My mother and I would have made a space for him in our car. She would have given him some plastic bags for his things. We would have opened the car door and asked, When are you moving in?

My mother had not given me much, had not bought me much of anything, but she'd filled me up with her words and songs. I was an encyclopedia of her chatter and young-mother hopes. From A to Z, I'd speak her. Her vowels and consonants would sing along with me forever and ever and ever after.

chatter quick or idle talk

The moment I looked into Mr. Brodsky's face, I wanted to run out and buy Band-Aids.

21

Eli's small black gun lay between two blouses. It was the first thing I looked for as I rummaged through the duffel bag. I hid it under the pillow on my bed.

My possessions from the dump – the marbles, bag of mercury, bullet, and buttons – I put away in the top drawer of the dresser. I hung up my clothes and placed my underwear and T-shirts in another drawer. I didn't have much. I didn't know where to put my drawing of the solar system, so I just rolled it up into a ball and threw it into the trash. I no longer needed to learn that Mercury was the closest planet to the sun and was on fire. I knew it.

I was organizing my things but I was really praying I'd find a cigarette. In a kind of frenzy, I was looking through every plastic bag and every pocket of my clothes. April May would say I needed to pray to the cigarette god.

I found one. It was a Mexican Marlboro Red from Corazón and Ray's trailer. Actually, the miracle was, I didn't find one cigarette, I found a whole pack. This was perfect proof that the cigarette god cared deeply about orphaned girls.

I walked over to the window, pushed the pale lace curtains to one side, pulled the blue Bic lighter out of my back pocket, and lit up. I took a deep drag and felt everything in me settle. The river of my blood grew calm.

I looked out over the garden and its tall oak trees and freshly cut lawn. There was one magnolia tree covered with the large white flowers that were just beginning to turn brown at the edges. Behind the trees, closer to the street, I could clearly see the playhouse made of wood and painted white. It had a small porch and two windows.

I'd taken only a few puffs when two children walked into the garden, down the path, and toward the front door. They were a white boy and a black girl. Through the smolder of my Marlboro, I could see the boy was dressed in blue jean shorts and had long, curly light-brown hair that was messy and grew down to his shoulders. He was tall and skinny and walked in long strides. The little girl beside him skipped and ran as she tried to keep up. She had a short Afro pinned in places with yellow and orange hair clips.

The boy stopped fast and looked up at the window. The little girl kept moving forward until she realized he was no longer walking toward the front door. She followed his gaze up to where I stood with my upper body leaning out the window as I sent a smoke plume skyward through my chimney-mouth.

to rummage through sth. *durchwühlen, durchstöbern*

dresser (*US*) *Frisierkommode*

trash (*US*) waste paper basket

orphan a child whose parents are dead

Bic company that makes cheap, mass-produced ballpoint pens

porch *(US) Veranda*

Afro African hairstyle with thick bushy curls

gaze looking at sb./sth. for a long time, esp. in surprise or admiration

plume of smoke a thin mass of smoke

I knew they were Leo and Helen. We looked at one another for a moment and then they continued into the house. Nobody waved. I finished my cigarette, stubbed it out on the windowsill, and threw the butt down into the garden below.

windowsill *Fensterbrett*

I was trying to decide if I should just light up another cigarette, as there was nothing else to do, when I heard a knock.

I walked across the room and opened the door.

For the first time, I knew the experience of opening a door, of standing, turning a knob and opening, opening, opening. Living in the car, because of the windows, we always knew who we opened a door to. This time, I didn't know who knocked behind the heavy oak wood.

I opened the door and it was Leo. He stood there chewing on the sleeve of his shirt.

Leo stood under the doorframe and stared at my face. I looked back into his light-brown eyes.

At my mother's university of love she'd learned about love at first sight. She said it was the only truth, and that love at first sight was like an accident. When I looked at Leo for the first time from my window I knew my arm was broken. I'd fallen down all the stairs. A train was coming down the tracks. And because I was so sad, I knew I loved him.

Are you an albino? Leo asked. A real albino?

No.

Are you sure?

Yes. I think so.

Where are you from? When did you get here?

Leo didn't give me time to answer. As with so many people, he was interested in the way I looked above all.

Did you know that in Tanzania witch doctors attack albinos?

No, I didn't know.

They think albino body parts bring good luck. Albinos have to hide in Tanzania, Leo said.

One of his eyes was a lazy eye, so it looked at me and then drifted away and seemed to look past me and out the window.

No. I didn't know this. I'm not an albino. I'm just me.

Leo walked into my room and sat on my bed. When Leo spoke he took the cuff out of his mouth. When he listened to my answers to his questions, he chewed on it again. The sleeve went in and out.

cuff *Ärmelaufschlag*

I was to learn that the left sleeves on all his shirts were worn and some even had holes from the gnawing of his teeth. This was a side effect produced by the Rivotril he took for anxiety.

to gnaw to bite or chew sth. repeatedly
Rivotril medication to prevent panic attacks or seizures

Is it strange to look how you look? he asked.

I don't know.

Come here and sit with me, he ordered. Come here.

I obeyed and sat next to him on the bed.

What happened to you? he asked. Why are you here?

I don't have anywhere to go. My mother was shot. She's dead.

Leo shook his head. Yes, I imagined that's what happened, he said. I'm a shoot too. So is Helen.

I wondered what he would think if he knew there was a gun under my pillow, right there, between us.

I'm seventeen. Well, almost eighteen, Leo said. How old are you?

I'm fourteen. Almost fifteen.

What about your father? Where's he?

I don't have a father. I never met him anyway.

As we sat on the edge of the bed, side by side, our clothes touched. My sleeve touched his sleeve and we knew it was our skin beneath the fabric that was touching.

fabric *Gewebe*

Did you know there are two bullets for every person in the world? Leo said.

No. Are you sure?

I know. I read about it. Everyone knows it. It's a fact, Leo said.

Then, if it's the case, I think my mother was shot with some bullets that belonged to other people.

Leo looked at me. His lazy eye looked down at my hands that were folded in my lap. I didn't know if I should look into his one eye or follow the look of his other eye down to my hands.

My blouse continued to touch his shirt and I felt Leo's warmth through the cotton.

You'll get used to my eye, he said. Everyone does. I was supposed to have an operation years ago, but it hasn't happened. The other people I was living with made an appointment but then it was canceled and then I moved here.

to cancel to call off

In a robotic, monotonous way, like saying times tables by heart, Leo told me his story. A foster child tells their story hundreds of times.

My mother used to say that some lives could be described in one book and others needed a whole encyclopedia. She would have said Leo's life needed only one sentence.

So, when Leo said he was an only child and that his mother had killed his father and then shot herself, he could have been saying two times two is four, four times four is sixteen.

When did this happen? I asked.

One of his eyes was looking at my mouth and the other eye looked into my left eye.

When I was four years old, he said. I don't remember my parents. I know my father was a doctor and my mother was a nurse. He was a heart surgeon. I know this from my file. He invented some-

heart surgeon *Herzchirurg*

thing for the heart. It was a valve or stent. It means I'm going to be rich when I turn eighteen.

There was no family for you? No one to take you?

Leo shook his head.

I don't even have a cousin, I said. Almost everyone at least has a cousin.

Do you want to see my room? he asked. Do you like to listen to music? Come, follow me. Do you know how to do origami?

Leo stood up and I followed him to his room, which was directly across from mine.

Leo had bins full of Lego and stacks of boxes with Mindstorms and robotics projects. He'd made complicated robots powered by batteries as well as helicopters and several rockets and what he called alien aircraft or UFOs.

Leo's room was decorated exactly like mine except that it was filled with his things and he even had two posters stapled to the wall. One was a poster of a solar eclipse and the other was a large photograph of Albert Einstein.

Pearl, Leo said. If there is anything that I have and you want it, you can have it. I don't want you to want something. It's awful to be wanting and wanting. Is there anything here, any of my things, you want? What's mine is yours.

He looked straight into my eyes.

When Leo said, What's mine is yours, his mismatched eyes aligned.

He could see my severe and strict soldier control over tears.

He could see my love-at-first-sight pool of love for him.

He knew he'd better not dare me to do anything, because I'd do it.

I knew he was not a strong white flag of a person but was put together with scraps of Scotch tape and a few staples and glue.

My mother had taught me all the love songs and they were going to follow me everywhere. She would've said, All these songs are the chorus of your life.

I was singing, *Surrender is just a word, my word.*

valve a device that controls the flow of liquid or air; *Ventil*
stent a long thin object put inside a tube in the body, for example, a blood vessel, so that its walls stay firm or so that body fluids can flow easily through it

origami *Papierfaltkunst*

Lego Mindstorms a software platform for the construction of programmable robots

solar eclipse *Sonnenfinsternis*

to align to put two or more things into a straight line

scrap a small piece of sth.
staple *Heftklammer*
glue *Klebstoff*

22

Helen was even smaller standing beside me than she'd seemed when I looked down at her from my window. I knew she was eight, but she looked about five.

Helen smiled. She smelled like burned marshmallows. I knew that smell so well. In the car, as we didn't have a stove or fireplace, we used to toast our marshmallows with a lighter.

Helen talked nonstop. It took me only a few minutes to realize that Helen had no idea who she was or where she came from. She said she had a white mommy and a black mommy. Then she said she had ten brothers and eleven sisters. She said she lived here and there near a beach and near a park. She was from Ethiopia and Finland. She was born in a house. She was born in a hospital. Helen had a twin brother and sister and she had two twin sisters. She had been in Catholic homes, Mormon homes, and Jehovah's Witness homes.

Helen was the true-blue foster child – too many homes, too many people, too many changes. Nobody had taught her not to pick her scabs. Nobody had taught her how to pull her baby teeth out with string.

scab *Wundschorf*

Helen had stayed in homes where she was given only cereal to eat. She'd been to homes where she had to reuse dental floss and tea bags and was given one square of toilet paper a day. Helen had been to foster homes where she slept on the floor in a hallway.

Helen often spoke to herself in the third person. Nobody corrected her.

Helen said, Helen has no maple flavoring. Helen is always dreaming of a white Christmas in Florida and she doesn't drink enough water. Helen loves forehead kisses. She sometimes wants to sleep forever and would not mind being pregnant. Helen feels better after a shower and she knows if you have bugs in your clothes just put them in a microwave oven. That kills all bugs even bed bugs.

maple *Ahorn*

bugs *Ungeziefer*
bed bug *Bettwanze*

Leo just accepted her chatter and I ended up doing the same. There was no way to follow her and attempt to make sense of her life.

Leo said, Show Pearl your collection of telephones.

Helen went to her room and came back in a minute with a plastic supermarket bag and dumped the contents out on the floor. She had at least seventeen phones and chargers in her bag.

Every foster home she goes to, they give her a phone and tell her to keep in touch. Leo said, There're so many now, Helen has no idea if they work or what house they belong to. I promised her I'll try and sort it out one day.

Yes, Helen said. These are the phones to all of Helen's houses.

What will you do with them? I asked.

Call on a phone to people in her family that's all and yes, of course, her friends Lulu, Gina, and Romey, Helen said. She wants to call her best friends to talk about things like, you know, do you like cats? Questions like that. A lot of people like cats. They're cute. Soft. Helen likes them a lot.

I'll figure it out for you, Leo said. First we're going to have to charge them all. Pearl will help us.

Then he went back to chewing his sleeve as he looked at the tangle of wires and multiple chargers.

Yes, of course I'll help, I said.

Helen crawled over to where I was sitting on the floor and sat very close to me. She rubbed her forehead against my upper arm. Hey, Helen said. You smell like bug-off.

I still smelled like the Mercury. The Raid was deep in my skin.

Maybe these conversations all happened over several days. I don't remember. There are only two things I know for sure happened on my first day. I found Leo and I also found out I would not have to worry about cigarettes.

At dinner that first night, Mr. Brodsky said, Pearl, you've been smoking, right?

Yes.

I can smell it.

Yes, yes, I answered, because I'd never been a liar. I was not raised up to deceive. My mother always said that a liar never recovers, never gets better, never gives it up and, if I looked around I'd see, there was no AA for liars.

Do you smoke a lot? Mr. Brodsky asked.

Whenever I can.

Don't worry, Mr. Brodsky said. If you want cigarettes I'll get them for you. You're a little girl whose mother just died so, if you want cigarettes, you can have them.

What brand do you like?

Camels.

Camels it is, he said.

The cigarette god was giving me faith.

tangle *Knäuel*

bug-off (*children's language*) insect repellent; *Mückenspray*

to deceive *täuschen*

AA (*abbr.*) Alcoholics Anonymous; an international self-help organization to fight alcoholism, founded in the USA in 1935

23

The first night at the foster home, rocks were thrown at my window. A night rainbow arched over the sky. Bullets fell instead of rain and Indian ghosts prowled outside in the garden, under the trees. I learned my lesson. This is the kind of dream you have if you sleep with a gun under your pillow.

to prowl *herumschleichen*

The next morning I awoke to the sound of Leo, Helen, and Mr. Brodsky getting ready to leave. Mr. Brodsky was helping Helen fix her hair. I could hear him asking what color hair clips she wanted.

Only yesterday I'd awoken in the car with my mother.

Only yesterday we'd said goodbye as I went off to school. She'd leaned against the Mercury in the lavender-colored nightgown as I walked away. The dump behind her was no longer a white mountain covered with hail.

My mother's last words were, You know, Pearl, when I played the piano God was there like a shadow.

Now it sounded like an omen and maybe every person's last words had importance. They were the full stop on a life.

When I heard Mr. Brodsky's car drive away with Leo and Helen, I tiptoed out of my room to go out on a field trip of the house.

field trip *Erkundungstour*

Leo's bedroom was ajar and so I looked inside.

ajar slightly open

His bed was unmade and in a mess. The pillow held the shape of Leo's head and the bottom bedsheet formed the imprint of his body.

I walked over and got inside the covers and placed my head where Leo's head had been. My cheek lay in the hollow mark of his cheek.

The warmth of his body was still inside the sheets and encircled me and warmed my legs and waist. I burrowed deep under the covers and breathed in his young-man-boy smell.

to burrow to move yourself into a position where you can feel, comfortable, warm and safe

I placed my hand under his pillow. In the cool cotton I found a round, old, hard pebble of chewing gum. It lay there like a pearl. I placed it in my mouth to taste him. A faint flavor of mint remained.

pebble a small, smooth round stone

I lay in Leo's bed as if I lay inside him.

The storm of tears came because I'd lost my mother, because a gun had killed her words, and because this was not in the Lamb's Book of Life.

24

Two days later a detective came to question me about my mother's death.

Mr. Brodsky let us sit in his study.

The detective was a black man with gray curly hair. His light-brown skin was covered in freckles and tiny dark moles. He had light-brown, droopy eyes.

mole small dark spot on a person's skin; *Muttermal*
droopy *herabhängend*

The man smiled with his mouth closed. He'd learned never to show his teeth to a scared girl.

I'm sorry about the loss of your mother, he said. I knew he'd said those words many times before because they sounded like a prayer you know by heart.

I'm sorry about your mother, he said again. And you know we really want to understand what happened. Do you mind talking to me?

No, I answered. I don't mind. The social worker said you'd be coming.

That's right, he said. So, did you know the kid who shot your mother?

Yes.

You sure.

Yes.

The detective took a photograph out from a file of papers he'd placed on the coffee table between us.

I'm sorry, he said. But could you look at his face just to make sure.

I looked at the photo of Mr. Don't Come Back. It was one of those high school graduation photos. He was wearing his graduation cap with the tassel falling to one side.

tassel *Bommel*

When I looked at his face, I remembered how my mother spoke about him. She said he was sweet and lost but that she knew he was also a firecracker you could burn your fingers on.

firecracker *Feuerwerkskörper*

Yes, I said. I've seen him. He stayed with us for two nights once. He was a runaway.

Okay, the detective said, and slipped the photograph back into his pile of papers. Can you think of any reason he might have wanted to kill your mother?

No, I said.

What about the Mexicans? the detective asked.

Corazón and Ray? They live in the trailer park. Do you mean Corazón and Ray?

Yes, those two. Were they up to anything suspicious?

No. What do you mean?

Were they selling? Heroin, you know. They're bringing it in from Mexico.

No. I don't know about that.
You sure? Was Ray around much?
No, not much. He had to go back and forth to Mexico all the time.
Now, the detective continued, I'd like to talk about Eli Redmond. Do you mind if we talk about him for a minute?
When the detective said Eli's name, I could hear my mother inside of me saying, Oh my baby, my baby, there are words that are so sharp you can cut yourself on them.
Who was Eli to your mother?
I could hear the whetstone grinding and honing Eli's name. I looked out the window toward the front garden. I didn't want to look into the detective's kind animal eyes that belonged to a deer or rabbit.

whetstone a stone used for sharpening the blades of knives
to grind (ground, ground) *mahlen*
to hone to make an object sharper

He was her boyfriend, I guess.
Did you know he was selling guns?
No. Not that. No. He was helping Pastor Rex get guns off the street. They were buying guns.
Okay, the policeman said. Yes, that's right.
The policeman reached over and placed his hand on my shoulder. It wasn't a light touch. He pressed with strength.
Listen, he said. We questioned Eli right after your mother was killed, but now we can't find him. If you see him or if he calls you, please let us know.
Yes, I said. You don't think Eli killed my mother, do you?
No. No. Of course not. And we know that boy was crazy. He had a history of paranoia. And with guns you're always in the wrong place at the wrong time.

paranoia an extreme and unreasonable feeling that other people do not like you or are going to harm or criticize you

The policeman stood up and reached into his wallet and gave me his card.
Call me, he said. If you remember something let me know. As I said, I'm sorry for your loss. Eli Redmond is wanted in five states in this country.
What for?
Killing a policeman. Armed robbery. Identity theft. You name it. And you can be sure his name is not Eli Redmond. He's a liar.
My mother knew it. I remembered the day in the car when I found her sitting in the backseat with her shoes on. She said she couldn't see inside of Eli. The windowpane of the man needed a wash.

identity theft the illegal use of another person's personal details, for example, in order to steal money from their bank account

windowpane *Fensterscheibe*

25

On those mornings after Leo, Helen and Mr. Brodsky left the house, I'd go and get into Leo's bed.

Every night Leo went to sleep in my my-mother-was-shot-and-killed tears.

Every day, alone in the house, I'd walk around and open drawers, run up and down the stairs, and lean against the walls. I wore the house like a dress.

In the kitchen I found a half-full box of Domino sugar cubes. This would have made my mother happy. I ate them all up in one morning.

Mr. Brodsky drove Helen and Leo to school and then he went to work. Later I learned that he was retired and was doing charity work at a nearby synagogue.

Leo had been with Mr. Brodsky for two years and Helen had been there for six months. This was unusual, because Mr. Brodsky was supposed to offer only temporary housing for emergency cases before the children moved to a more permanent foster home. Leo explained that as soon as Mr. Brodsky turned eighty years old, in only a few months, all three of us would be removed from his care because of his age.

Soon after my arrival at Mr. Brodsky's house, I was standing at my window, lighting up a Camel, when I saw the car drive up and park in the driveway. It was the social worker's car. She looked up and I quickly leaned away from the window, but she'd seen me. I threw my lit cigarette in the water glass by my bed and stood near the window. The car door opened and closed. I heard her footsteps as she walked toward the house.

She rang the doorbell.

I was going to be moved to another house. I knew it. I wanted to hide under my bed. I wanted to run away. I wanted to lock myself up in the room.

Leo and Helen explained to me that the worst thing about being a foster child was being moved from house to house and school to school.

Helen said, When you go, you see, you don't have a mommy, so everybody's clothes get mixed up. All these kids are wearing your T-shirt or you think it's yours but you don't know if you don't have your mommy to tell you. This girl, this girl who was always scratching me, she took my sweater and said it was her sweater but there was no mommy to say it was Helen's sweater.

Leo had been in one foster home where an older boy had hit him all the time. Leo used to stuff towels around the waist of his jeans and inside his sleeves so it wouldn't hurt as much.

Leo said, if you're a foster child and you have a fever, no one ever touches your forehead to feel your heat. All they do is hand you a thermometer.
Mr. Brodsky was the best foster parent they'd ever had.
Helen said Leo chewed his sleeves because he was scared he'd have to leave Mr. Brodsky. Leo said that Helen rocked back and forth all the time because she didn't want to leave this home. They knew each other better than a brother and sister.
After spending time with Leo and Helen and hearing their stories, I swore I'd run away before I was moved to another house.
The social worker rang the door bell again.
I walked down the stairs and opened the door.
The social worker wore the same suit she'd had on the week before.
The front door let in the garden smells. The scent of magnolia flowers, roses, and dew-wet grass blew into the house.
The social worker was holding a box in her hands and had a yellow manila envelope tucked under one arm.

manila envelope an envelope made of strong light-brown paper

So, are you talking these days? she asked.
Yes.
Are you getting along with the other shoots?
Yes.
Does Mr. Brodsky know you smoke? Where are you getting those cigarettes? I'll have to put in a report about this.
No, he doesn't know, I answered. They're mine. I brought them with me when I came here.
Well, I'm putting it in the report. You could burn this house down.
I'll stop, I said. I promise.
Addicts always say that. Do you know how many kids like you promise me they're going to give up drugs, like pot or heroin? Huh? Sure you're going to give up cigarettes. You think I can believe that? It's going in the report. It's against the law for you to smoke.
I'll stop, I said again. I promise.
Listen, she said. Maybe don't even bother to unpack. I hear that you're going to be moved to another home within a month. I've seen the paperwork. Don't get too comfortable.
I didn't answer.
And here, the social worker said. This is yours. They gave me these things to give to you. Here.
The box moved from her hands into my hands.
No, I said. You're mistaken. This box isn't mine. I've never seen it before. This is also for you, she said, and placed the yellow manila envelope on the hallway table. It's the coroner's report. The police said to hand these things over to you.

coroner *Gerichtsmediziner*

What is it? I asked again.

Listen, Pearl, she said. I've got to go now. I'll be in touch. I'm sorry about all of this. I think the police made a mistake. You're not supposed to get these things until you turn eighteen, but who am I to get in an argument with the police? I follow orders. I'm not here to question.

I looked down at the box.

That box has your mother's ashes inside, so be careful with it, she said.

I didn't answer.

She walked out of the hallway and closed the front door behind her. The sweet garden air also left with her steps.

If Noelle had been there, she would have said, Mistakes and deaths come in threes.

If April May had been there with me, she would have said, Let's just go and throw it all away in some river. You cannot run around with that box.

If my mother had been with me she would have said, Go have a dream that I'm still alive. Go have a nap, sweet baby girl.

The manila envelope contained the small opal ring Mr. Rodrigo, the piano teacher, had given to my mother. I placed it, and all those Cuban superstitions, on my finger.

The envelope also contained the bullets.

The coroner and the police had sent me those twenty bullets as if they belonged to my mother because they were found inside her body. It was as if they were jewels. The bullets were my inheritance.

inheritance *Erbe*

26

For several weeks before my arrival, Mr. Brodsky had planned to take Helen and Leo to visit a circus museum, which was in Sarasota and only an hour's drive from the house. Mr. Brodsky said I didn't have to go but was welcome to go with them.

You have to come, Leo said, and so I went.

Leo sat in the front seat next to Mr. Brodsky and I sat in the back with Helen, who talked nonstop the whole way.

kite *Drachen, Papierdrachen*

Why are we interested in asking questions? Helen said. That's simple. Don't you want to know why a kite works? Or if black is a color or if white is a color? And what about the first question? Who thought about that first? And what about this? Has anybody heard footsteps outside our room at night and then you realize it's just your own heartbeat? Does anybody else confuse heartbeats with footsteps?

Mr. Brodsky, Leo, and I just let her talk. Helen was never looking for conversation.

The Ringling Museum was in a huge pink palace built by one of the Ringling brothers, who'd made his fortune from the circus. The building, which was a copy of a Venetian palace, also housed a great art collection.

stilts *Stelzen*

In the museum, Leo, Helen, and I walked together, looking at the small clown cars, wagons, a model of a woman on stilts whose head touched the ceiling, cannons that shot people into the air, and displays of circus costumes.

felt *Filz*

barber a man whose job is cutting men's hair

Ferris wheel *Riesenrad*

There was a model of a miniature circus made up of thousands of pieces. It re-created what the circus had been like when it traveled around the country by train. The model circus was laid out on display tables covered in green felt. It was so complete it even had the medical and barber tents on display. The reproductions of Ferris wheels and merry-go-rounds were electrically wired so they worked and went around and around. Helen was most fascinated by this, as it was all dollhouse-size and even had miniature circus people and animals.

Leo was beside me at all times because we knew walking close to someone you love never lasts.

ballyhoo *(sl.)* noise and tumult

freak abnormal

ostrich *der Vogel Strauß*

pincushion *Nadelkissen*

meat skewer *Fleischspieß*

Leo was most interested in the Ballyhoo posters. We learned that these were the free shows given outside a circus to attract a crowd and was also known as the freak show. Under the words 'Shocking' and 'Amazing' were drawings of the Frog Man, Birdlady, Bearded Woman, and Human Torso, which was a man without arms or legs. The Human Ostrich was a man who could swallow anything, including lightbulbs and knives. The Human Pincushion was an act where the performer pushed hatpins, meat skewers, and needles into his flesh.

The Sword Swallower, who swallowed not only swords, mesmerized Leo. The performer also ingested fly swatters, neon tubes, rifle barrels, and coat hangers.

On one wall there was a poster of Siamese twins. I stopped and stared at the images of the original conjoined twins called Chang and Eng.

I've seen real Siamese twins, I said to Leo. They were alligators. They were born on our beach right on the river.

As I looked into the Asian faces of Chang and Eng Bunker, who were joined at the chest, I remembered the day my mother and I had walked hand in hand to the river to look at the baby alligators. The odors of the dump came to me with the memory, along with the recollection of clouds of blue-and-yellow dragonflies that lived near our river. I was glad my mother wasn't here because I knew that her ability to see into people's pain and the freak show were a bad mix. I, who'd inherited this trait, had to stand in front of almost every poster about the freaks with my eyes closed.

Why don't you look? Leo asked.

He still didn't know everything about me.

Mr. Brodsky liked the reproduction of a painting of Tom Thumb and his wife when they appeared at a formal reception in London standing like salt and pepper shakers on a table, dressed in tails and a gown.

In the museum shop there were postcards of the image for sale.

Kids, would you like a postcard? he asked.

When Mr. Brodsky called the three of us kids we felt like we were part of a family and belonged. That word was a blanket tucked around us.

Every once in a while Mr. Brodsky would say something important that I wanted to remember, but it always began with the word 'kids.'

Once at dinner he said, Kids, death is the place of the unknown but you should know the unknown is also here on Earth.

Of course we know this, Mr. Brodsky, Helen answered. Everyone knows this. It is not any kind of a new idea.

As we drove back home from the circus museum we were quiet inside the car. Leo, Helen, and I had been on a Saturday-afternoon outing. We were in a car driving home to a meal of hamburgers and ice cream with cones. On that night we were going to sleep in bedrooms in beds with white cotton sheets.

Leo, Helen, and I were quiet in the car on the drive home because we were in the perfect childhood dream of companionship and safety.

And on that afternoon the dream was in the real world. We knew that for one day we'd crossed over.

sword [sɔːd]
to mesmerize *jdn. faszinieren*
to ingest sth. to eat or drink sth.

Tom Thumb a 1621 English fairy tale about Tom, who is the size of his father's thumb and experiences many adventures
shaker *Streuer*
tails *Frack*
gown *Abendkleid*

to tuck sth. around sb. *jdn. behaglich in etw. einpacken*

ice cream cone *Eishörnchen*

27

Chesed Shel Emet a society founded by Jewish immigrants in order to bury their deceased according to Jewish rituals
trowel *Schaufel*
rake *Harke*

I chose the earth under the magnolia tree.
I only know how to do a Jewish burial, Mr. Brodsky said. It's the Chesed Shel Emet. This will be your last act of kindness toward your mother.
Mr. Brodsky gave me two trowels and a small rake and told Leo, Helen, and me to go to the garden and dig a hole deep and big enough to hold the box of ashes.
Pearl, Mr. Brodsky said, to bury someone is considered the greatest act of love.
The three of us walked out to the garden. The sky was a deep blue and streaked with the long white trails from airplanes. The white ribbons appeared and disappeared above us.
We knelt around the magnolia tree. I handed the rake to Helen and the trowel to Leo.
You two start, I said.
I think this is a good place, Helen said. You'll always know where she is.

sniper *Heckenschütze*
randomly *wahllos*

Helen had no idea where her parents or her two siblings were buried. A sniper who'd shot at people randomly in a park had killed her family. It was even in the news, Leo told me. He'd read all about it. The sniper was carrying many guns. He'd killed fourteen people before the police shot him.
Helen wasn't shot, as she had been inside her baby carriage and, because of this, had been in foster care ever since. She knew her family had been from Miami and insisted she remembered her family and even knew what they looked like, but Leo and I knew this was impossible. Helen was going to get the family's belongings when she turned eighteen and hoped there might be photographs in those things.
Leo and Helen began to dig.
So, what was she like, your mother? Helen asked as she held the rake in her small hand and began to scrape the top layer of grassy dirt off my mother's grave.
I lay down on the grass beside the tree and looked up at the sky, towards the streaks left by the airplanes.
She was just a mother. Nobody knows me anymore, I answered.
No one ever knew me, Helen said. Was she pretty?
She could play the piano. She knew how to speak French.
Did she look like you?
She was a little like me, but not pale the way I am.
Did you know that man who killed her?
No. He was a stranger.

I wasn't going to fill Helen's mind up with Mr. Don't Come Back.
I picked up a trowel.
So what does that word 'foster' really mean? Helen asked.
She could never stop talking.
Foster home? she said. Foster care? What's foster? What's the word? What does 'foster' mean? I just don't get it.
After a while, Mr. Brodsky came outside wearing a shawl over his shoulders. In his hands he held the box with my mother's ashes and a prayer book. He also carried two small dark-blue Kippahs for Leo and him to wear.
Helen, Leo, and I stood around the small grave in the garden while Mr. Brodsky placed the box inside the freshly dug hole. Then we all took turns throwing handfuls of dirt over the box while Mr. Brodsky read a prayer aloud.
He said, Exalted and hallowed be God's great name in the world that God created, according to a plan. May God's majesty be revealed in the day of our lifetime and the life of all Israel – speedily, imminently, to which we say Amen.
Once the box was buried, Helen said we had to buy some flowers to plant there.
Is there anything you want to say? Mr. Brodsky asked me.
I shook my head, but inside I was hearing the songs, my mother's songs, the chorus-of-my-life songs.
After the burial, Helen and Mr. Brodsky went back to the house. He tutored Helen in math on the weekends. She skipped circles around him as he walked. We could hear her nonstop chatter as they walked away. Helen was asking, Do you believe in heaven, Mr. Brodsky, sir? I do. It just has to be. It has to be. Otherwise why's there a sky, sir? Why?
Let's go to the playhouse, Leo said.
I never said no to him. Loving him meant saying yes.
The playhouse was made of wood and painted white and had two windows. Inside there was a living room with two small, child-sized chairs and a kitchen area with furniture made out of wood. The stovetop burners were painted red to look as if they were lit. The playhouse also had a small bathroom and a bedroom with a short single bed in it. Both the kitchen and the bathroom had running water. Leo and I washed off my mother's grave dirt in the small kitchen sink and shook our hands dry in the air.
To one side of the sink there were two cans of tuna fish, a half-eaten loaf of bread, a small jar of mayonnaise. There were also two small boxes of Corn Flakes.
In the bathroom there was a toothbrush and a small tube of toothpaste.
Do you think someone's living here? I asked Leo.

Kippah a cap worn by Jewish men

to exalt to praise
to hallow *als heilig verehren*
to reveal sth. to make sth. known

imminently very soon

to skip circles *im Kreis hüpfen*

stovetop burner *Brenner an einem Gasherd*

jar (glass) container

No, it's just Helen. She likes to come here and bring stuff, he said. She thinks the playhouse is hers. I never come here.

Leo and I lay down on the playhouse play bed. It was small, so we couldn't stretch out completely and had to pull our knees up. Sunlight came in through the window and warmed our bodies. I lay my head on Leo's chest and listened to his heartbeat under the blue cotton shirt. Two plastic buttons pressed into my cheek.

He said, I love thinking about space.

What do you mean? I asked.

Big Bang the large explosion that many scientists believe created the universe

You know, everything that's being discovered. The Big Bang, new galaxies, all of that. The universe.

It's warm in here, I said. Do these windows open?

No. They don't open.

And we fell asleep in our little house, in our little bed under a little window.

to float *schweben*

In my dream the playhouse lifted up off the earth. It floated in the air toward the horizon and high above our new joyful sorrow.

28

In the evening, after my mother's funeral, I went into Mr. Brodsky's study for the first time. He was sitting at his desk reading the newspaper. His computer was also open and the light from the machine lit up Mr. Brodsky's face.

Give me a minute, he said. I want to finish this.

As he continued to read, I walked around the room and looked at the photographs that were on tables, bookshelves, and even hanging on the wall. The room was like a photography museum.

Mr. Brodsky folded his newspaper and looked up at me.

There're so many photographs, I said. Do you know all these people?

Yes, They're of my family. Some are old from far away, from Odessa, Ukraine. A few are from Berlin. I really should get rid of them all, he said. I've thought about it for a while now.

Why?

One of the things that are so troubling about old photographs is that you know what happened afterward. It's as if you look at the photo and then zoom, just like a movie, you know what's coming.

Mr. Brodsky stood up and walked over to where I stood. He picked up a photograph I was looking at.

So, he said. Here's a photo with my father and our new puppy. I'm about five years old there. I look happy with the dog. But I know that he then had to kill that dog because it learned to coax chickens into a corner and eat them. In that happy photo, we didn't know the movie that was coming. But when I look at the photo now, today, I know it's all going to go wrong with that dog.

to coax to persuade someone gently to do something or go somewhere, by being kind and patient, or by appearing to be

I don't have any photographs. Well, I need to look through my mother's bag. Maybe I'll find some there, I said.

You will learn. You'll see the happy photograph and then, in your mind, you will see the movie that comes afterward.

The killing?

Yes.

So there is no such thing as a happy photograph?

I don't think so. No.

29

Only three weeks after I'd been left at Mr. Brodsky's house, I heard someone ring the bell at the front door. My first thought was that the social worker had come to take me to another foster home. Every day I dreaded this.

to dread sth. to feel extremely worried about sth.
chore [tʃɔ:r] *Routinehausarbeit*

I was alone in the basement doing the laundry. This was a chore that Mr. Brodsky had given me, as he liked everyone who stayed at this house to help out with something.

I liked to sit in the warm basement and look into the round port-hole window of the washing machine. There in the ocean of blue Tide and water I'd watch my clothes mix with Leo's clothes through the wash and rinse and spin cycles.

Tide brand name of a US laundry detergent like the German detergent *Persil*

When I moved the clothes to the dryer, I'd never untie my blouses that were knotted up with his shirts. I always folded his clothes with care, even pressing them with my hands, so at least there would be devotion in the clothes that held his body.

devotion loyalty, love or care for sb./sth.

I walked upstairs and opened the front door.

It was Corazón.

She opened her arms and took me into her and held me tight as if I were her own lost child.

She said, Mi niña, my poor child, my baby girl.

niña Spanish for girl

But I pushed away from her, because I was not hers and I knew I wasn't belonging to anyone. There was no comfort beyond warm clothes. People feeling sorry for me was going to make me feel like spitting.

I closed the front door and let her into the kitchen.

How did you find me? I asked as she sat down on one of the chairs that circled the round breakfast table.

Corazón was all made up, as always. She even had her false eye-lashes on. Her long, fake fingernails were painted red and had a perfect white dot in the middle of each nail. Her black hair was streaked with blond and she was wearing light-pink lipstick.

Corazón said, Mi niña, I came to get you away from this horrible place. This house, she's not for you.

How did you find me?

Muñeca, let's go and see Selena's grave. We have to go and take her some flowers. They killed your mama just like they killed Selena. Don't tell me this is a coincidence.

muñeca (*coll.*) Spanish for darling

Corazón reached for my hand across the table to hold it in hers, but I pulled away and placed my hands in the pockets of my jeans. Just because my mother was dead, it didn't mean I needed my hand held to cross the street.

Corazón leaned back in her chair and looked at me as if she were fitting me for a dress. The ribbon of measuring tape was in her eyes.

She said, Pearl, it's gun love. That's what the man felt for your mother. He bought that gun and didn't even know it was for her until he saw her. So you must think of it as a sacrifice. Life is always on the edge of death. It was a good day to die. God knows: I would hear and would be heard, I would be wounded and I would wound, I would be saved and I would save. I have the bus tickets to Texas. We're going to Corpus Christi and we're taking some flowers for Selena's grave. You're coming.

sacrifice *Opfer*

Yes, I said.

I knew you would never say no to this.

As she was speaking, I knew I'd rather run off with her than be taken off to some other foster-care home. It was only a matter of days. I wasn't going to become Helen or Leo and march in a band for somebody.

to march in a band here: to protest in support of sth.

I looked at Corazón and I saw my escape road away from a daisy chain of foster homes.

daisy chain *Gänseblümchenkette*; here: a long row

The Risk Star was shining bright above the foster home.

Where's Ray? I asked.

That stupid Ray. He disappeared. He's so lazy. He's so damn lazy, when he goes to pick the oranges, we will already be drinking the juice. You know! And Eli and Pastor Rex – those two rats – they got out of there before your mother was even taken away. She was still warm, almost alive, you could say. Well, like a rose is alive in a vase. Not really.

vase [vɑːz]

How did you find me?

Listen, Pearlita, I always say: if Ray dies tonight, I'll take my time getting there to say goodbye to him. Let him wait for my tears!

How did you find me?

Noelle told me. Your social worker told her mama where you'd be for the next few weeks in case someone showed up looking for you, like an aunt or cousin.

Where are you staying? I asked.

I've spent these last nights, all weekend sleeping in that estúpido little playhouse in the garden and eating tuna fish.

That man never left the house so I could go and see you.

I was quiet for a minute. I looked at Corazón and knew everything she said was true. She was not going to give me away to the United States of America fate. She was betting on Mexican love.

Maybe it's better than living in a car, I said, and smiled.

I don't know how you and Margot survived that. Well, I guess she didn't.

Corazón told me that everyone at the trailer park was still there except for Pastor Rex and Eli. She said that on the day my mother had been killed both men had disappeared and had not returned.

Pastor Rex? I asked. Why did he leave?

And Corazón explained it all.

Pastor Rex, well, who knows if he's even a pastor, she said. I do doubt it. He, Eli, and Ray have worked for years in the south of Texas and Florida getting guns to sell in Mexico.

I wasn't surprised, because there was no surprise left in me. I'd used it up.

She also told me that only two days after I left, our car had been hauled away from the visitors' parking area.

It was so fast, Corazón said. It was suddenly gone.

I wonder where they took it.

After the car was taken, everyone was there, walking around where our car had been parked, Corazón said. I found a complete roll of Life Savers there. I didn't pick them up as they'd probably been there for ten years.

She made me laugh.

There was also a bullet there, under the car in the grass, Corazón said. I didn't pick that up either.

I knew that was the bullet which my mother and I had looked for. It was the bullet that had left a clean hole in the car with a dark ring of residue.

When I thought of our car being towed away, I remembered sleeping in the backseat with my mother while Mr. Don't Come Back slept in my place. He'd been the only person who'd shared that car with us and knew what it was like to sleep in the dark Mercury with the taste of Raid on one's mouth. My mother and I didn't know we'd invited our fate in to receive our homeless hospitality.

hospitality the act of being friendly and welcoming to guests and visitors

And that Sergeant Bob, Corazón continued, he said people get killed all the time and that it's just not news. And all he was saying is that your mama was the albatross. That bird.

And what did April May say?

I don't remember. Noelle said she'd seen everything, but she didn't tell that to the police. Mrs. Roberta didn't want that loca Noelle talking to policemen, as she'd get her story all mixed up. That Noelle said midnight is knocking.

loca Spanish for mad woman

When Corazón came, I didn't hesitate to say yes. I was leaving. But first I needed to do something. I told her we'd leave in two days.

It's going to be special to see Selena's grave. It will be almost like being with her, Corazón said.

Corazón knew everything about the story. She knew Yolanda Saldívar, Selena's manager and her killer, always claimed that the gun accidentally went off. Corazón had read this was impossible, as the .38-caliber revolver required eleven pounds of pressure on the trigger to fire. That kind of pressure is no accident, Corazón said.

When I spent time with Corazón in her trailer cleaning the guns, Corazón said, On March thirtieth, 2025, when Yolanda gets out of jail, I'm going to be there. I will be there standing at the prison gate. What are you going to say to her? I asked.

I don't know yet. I'm figuring it out.

You're not going to kill her?

I won't have to, niña. Someone else will take care of that job. Maybe I'll just ask her why the hell she just didn't slap Selena across the face like a good Latina. Why did she have to kill her? Who kills a nightingale? I want to hear her answer to that.

nightingale *Nachtigall*

You must be hungry. What do you want for breakfast? I asked.

She's a beautiful kitchen, Corazón said, and stood up and caressed the black-and-white marble counters. Then she opened up one of the cupboards and looked inside.

Look at all this chocolate and boxes of cookies, she said. I want to eat everything in here.

I helped her around the kitchen and watched her cook up some scrambled eggs. I prepared her a glass of orange juice. From freshly squeezed oranges.

I'm going to bathe too, she said. I haven't bathed in days. There's no shower in that playhouse.

Yes, of course, I said. I'll get you some clean towels.

If you're raised up in a car you'll give anyone the chance to have a shower.

The house smells like orange flowers, Corazón said. Did you notice that?

No, I said.

Well, it does. Someone sprinkles orange flower water all over the place.

After she'd finished eating breakfast, I took her to my room and then she had a long shower.

While she was bathing I took the gun out from under my pillow, where it had been since the day I'd arrived, and placed it in one of the dresser drawers.

When Corazón got out of the shower she lay on the bed wrapped in the large, white towel and fell asleep.

I sat in the chair at the window and looked at Corazón's kind face.

She'd saved me from the girl-without-a-friend loneliness of the empty trailer full of guns, and now Corazón was going to save me from being in the we-don't-want-you-here foster-child life.

When Corazón woke up and opened her big brown eyes, she sat up straight and patted the bed with the palm of her hand and said, Come sit next to me.

I stood up and sat next to her and she wrapped her arms around me. She caressed my hair and kissed my cheek and forehead. She rocked me back and forth in her rocking-chair body. I let her treat me like a doll.

Do you have a cigarette for me? she asked.

Of course, I said.

We sat, side by side, with the covers over our legs, smoking the cigarettes.

You know you're not supposed to smoke in bed, Corazón said.

Yes, I know.

Well, just as long as you're not supposed to, then you can do it. It's like I know I'm not supposed to eat a lot of sugar. Well, I know I shouldn't do it and then I do it. Does a doctor really think you're not going to eat ice cream? That's so ridiculous, it's ridiculous.

Corazón, I said. My mother is buried out there in the garden. She's in a box under the magnolia tree. What do you think?

It's the perfect place. Your mother would have loved this house.

Yes, I said. But I'm not sure about being buried in a place you don't know.

Well, it happens all the time because you're never really in charge of what happens to your body – not even when you're alive.

Greyhound Lines American intercity coach service with about 3,800 destinations across the USA

Corazón wanted to leave and get on the road as soon as possible. We were going to take the Greyhound bus all the way to Texas. She had it all planned out.

I needed two days to do everything. It was Monday. I told her we'd leave on Thursday. She could spend the afternoons, when Mr. Brodsky was home, in the playhouse. I'd give her some cookies and apples. I promised I would sneak her in at night so she could sleep in my bed with me.

I want you to meet Helen and Leo, I said.

Oh no. They'll tell. They'll tell that man that you're leaving with me.

to rat on sb. (*phr. v., sl., disapproving*) to be disloyal to sb., especially by giving away secret information about them

No, I said. Foster children never rat on anyone. That's the golden foster-child rule.

Are you sure?

Yes. Leo told me. He said the first thing foster children learn to say is, I didn't see a thing.

On Monday night, after everyone had gone to sleep, I went downstairs, opened the front door, and ran out into the garden. I walked past my mother's grave. Around me was the sound of crickets and a soft humming of other insects.

cricket *Grille*

When I reached the playhouse, Corazón opened the small door and stepped out. I took her hand and we walked back to the house and up to my room.

We lay in bed in the dark and listened to the sounds outside and inside and the sound of each other breathing.

How do you feel? Are you okay? Corazón asked.

I cannot find the words.

I'm not in a hurry. Look for the words.

I slipped out of the bed and opened the curtains and then the window. A cold night breeze blew into the smoky room. I looked down at the garden and at the place my mother's ashes were buried. A cloud of fireflies lit up the garden with tiny flashes everywhere.

I left the window open and got back into bed.

After a while Corazón whispered, Do you think this señor here has some money we could take? We could use some more money.

I don't know, I whispered back. Leave it to me. After Mr. Brodsky and Leo and Helen leave tomorrow morning, I'll check around.

Okay, buenas noches.

Corazón?

Yes, What is it?

What do you think happened to my mother?

What do you mean?

How did all this happen to us?

What?

My mother never should have let Eli into our car. She should've rolled up the window.

Your mother wanted to be rescued, Corazón said. She had no family, no house, no roof. How can anyone live in a car for all those years? She was a lonely woman. That man just walked into her and sat down.

Yes, I said. I do know what happened. She wanted every day to be a Sunday. That's a song. She wanted a Sunday kind of love.

30

On Tuesday, while Leo, Helen, and Mr. Brodsky were away and Corazón had gone off to buy our Greyhound bus tickets, I sat on the bed and opened up all my mother's plastic bags.

There was a bag of hair clips, nail clippers, and nail files. There were two bags filled with bras and underpants. There was a bag with shorts and skirts. One bag was full of nail-polish bottles.

I'd watched my mother organizing these bags over and over again throughout my life. Now I knew that she was trying to create the logic of a closet and a set of drawers out of supermarket bags.

One of the last bags had the pair of white gloves in it. The last time I'd seen them, we'd been at church. I'd watched as, with care, she'd peeled the gloves off her small, childlike hands so she could play the piano and then handed them to me. I could hear F minor as if the music was in the lace. I rolled up the gloves into a ball as if they were tissues and tossed them into the trash by my bed.

tissue soft paper used for cleaning; *Papiertaschentuch*

As I looked through her clothes, I checked her pockets, which all contained sharp stones or pieces of glass. Everywhere my mother walked she anticipated that someone might be out walking barefoot so she always picked up those objects and put them into her pockets. She kept people she didn't even know safe.

The last bag I opened contained the testimony of her childhood and wealthy upbringing. Here were things she'd never used once in our trailer park and she did not have time to sell along with everything else. There was a small black silk clutch with ruby-colored beads sewn all over the outside and a jar containing ten pearl buttons each circled by a trim of tiny rhinestones.

clutch *Unterarmtasche ohne Griffe oder Tragegurt*
to sew (sewed, sewn) [səʊ] *nähen*
trim *Einfassung*
rhinestone *Glaskristallstein*

There were no bags with photographs or important documents. There was not a single piece of paper that might have told me who we were. Her teenage-runaway motherhood did not think of those kinds of things.

I picked up all the bags and placed them in a heap right next to the wastepaper basket by the small desk. No one else was ever going to remember my mother. It was up to me to keep her alive inside of me. So I closed my eyes and listened and my mother said, I never would have known better because Eli's hands were soap and I needed a good washing.

Tuesday night Corazón slept in my bed again. She said she had the tickets.

It's going to be a long trip, she said. We're going to see parts of the United States we've never heard of before. I just pray to God no policeman looks at us and wonders what this Latina is doing with a white girl. You don't even look fourteen. If I saw you at the bus station, I'd think you were nine or ten. When are you going to start growing some breasts? Do you menstruate yet?

Yes, of course I do, I said. I'm not stupid.

What does that have to do with being stupid?

I don't know.

On Wednesday Corazón spent the whole day in the playhouse because that was the only day of the week the cleaning lady came to the house.

I went to Mr. Brodsky's studio to look for a pair of scissors. I found a large pair on his desk next to a letter opener and three pencils. I picked up the scissors and took them up to my room.

I untied the yellow ribbon and opened the silk box and took out my grandmother's wedding dress. I placed it on the bed and pressed it out with the shirt pulled open wide and the sleeves drawn down on each side. The waist was cinched with a white satin ribbon that tied in a bow at the back.

Then I lay down the dress.

The silk chiffon was soft and a smell seemed to burst out of the fabric. It was a scent of old perfume and of old times. My mother and everything in the past smelled of patchouli.

Near the collar I could see a tiny stain of pale pink makeup. On the hem, on the front of the long skirt, there was a small tear and a little piece of caked, dried mud. It was as if someone had stepped on her dress while she was dancing. The bride was gone but the evidence of the dance was still in the dress.

As Mr. Brodsky had said earlier, I knew what happened after this wedding even if I didn't have a photograph. When my grandmother wore the dress she didn't know the car crash with the Pepsi truck was coming. She never knew that her teenage daughter would have run away from fly swatters and gas-stove dreams with a newborn.

Once I had measured the length of my body by lying down on top of the dress. I stood and cut up the garment with the scissors. I sliced off at least five inches from the sleeves and twelve inches off the hem.

That night I went to Leo's room with Helen. I told them both Corazón had come for me and that I was running away with her the next day.

Leo, I want to marry you before I leave, I said.

He said, Yes.

I'd known it for a long time: those three letters were the best letters of the alphabet.

After Mr. Brodsky had gone to sleep, Leo, Helen, and I went out to the garden to get Corazón from the playhouse.

to cinch *umwickeln*
bow [baʊ] *Schleife*

scent a pleasant natural smell
patchouli *Patschulikraut*
collar *Kragen*
hem *Saum*

evidence *Hinweis, Beleg*

garment piece of clothing
to slice to cut into sth. with a sharp knife
inch a unit for measuring length; 1 inch = 2.54 cm

Helen thought it was wonderful that Corazón had been living in there.
Really, Helen said, all those tuna cans were yours? Really?
Yes, I had to buy something that wouldn't spoil and I even hate tuna fish, Corazón said. Who was the idiot who invented that horrible food? It's really cat food.
Oh yes! Helen said. It's cat food!
I could see that Helen and Corazón had fallen in love with each other. Corazón was already thinking about combing Helen's knot-filled Afro and rubbing her dry little-girl skin with lemons. Helen was just itching to crawl onto Corazón's lap and fall asleep. She also kept looking at Corazón's painted fingernails. Finally, Helen asked, Why, lady, do you have a white dot in the middle of each nail?
Those are stars, little girl, Corazón said. I caught them from the sky and they stuck to my fingernails.
Helen wanted to believe her. She also decided she wanted to run away with us and I could see that Corazón was practically ready to leave me behind and take Helen instead.
No, Corazón said. Not this time. We'll come back and get you. I promise.
Leave us your phone number, Helen said.
Of course we will, I answered.
We closed the door behind us and left the playhouse.
If my mother were looking down from heaven, she would have seen four strays running across a garden late at night in search of a wedding.
I left Helen, Leo, and Corazón in Leo's room and went to my room to get ready.
Corazón had agreed to perform the ceremony. She said, Okay, I'll let you marry him because I'm a Catholic and Catholics accept any kind of thing because you can always confess and get absolved. Thank God. Why would anyone want to be any other religion?
Helen was going to be my bridesmaid.
In my room I put on the wedding dress. The silk chiffon felt soft and cold on my skin. Then I walked across the hall to Leo's bedroom.
As I stood in the doorway, Leo, Helen, and Corazón stared at me. They had not expected me to be wearing a real wedding dress.
Oh, no! I should have baked a cake, Corazón said, and shook her head.
You're real. You're really real, Pearl, Helen said. She ran over to me and rubbed her cheek against the cloth. Is this silk? Is this what spiders make?

knot *Knoten*
to itch here: to have a strong desire to do sth.
lap *Schoß*
to confess *beichten*
to get absolved *Vergebung (für Sünden) bekommen*
bridesmaid *Brautjungfer*

I don't have a ring, Leo said.

I have a ring, I said, and pulled my mother's small opal ring off my finger.

Corazón performed the ceremony in Spanish.

You know, it's just not born to me to say this in English. So. Like this. Now you say yes.

Leo placed the ring on my finger and he kissed my cheek.

That night Corazón slept alone in my bed, Helen went back to her room, and I stayed with Leo.

The chorus of my life that night was Leo's heartbeat.

I didn't know another body could make me feel protected. He was fleece and fur, apple rind and orange peel, eggshell, pod and bark, and bandage.

I'm dreaming you, he said again.

I hoped he was right. I hoped it was all the dream side.

We knew we were too young for our bodies.

fleece a thick covering of wool on a sheep
fur *Fell*
pod *Schote*
bark *Rinde*

31

lowdown rat (*sl.*) sb. who is dishonest, unfair, despicable

to dye sth. *etw. färben*

The next morning I went downstairs to say goodbye to Mr. Brodsky. Of course he didn't know I was saying goodbye forever. This did not make me feel like a lowdown rat.

I waved to Leo and Helen as they got in the car. They didn't wave back. Foster children don't wave goodbye. They forgot to tell me this.

Corazón made breakfast while I packed my things. I left Leo my objects from the dump and I left Helen my wedding dress.

The manila envelope, with the twenty bullets that had been shot into my mother's body, was still beside my bed. I packed the envelope in the duffel bag.

Eli's gun was in the top dresser drawer, where I'd kept it ever since Corazón had arrived.

I took out the weapon and held it in my hands.

The day Eli had given us the gun, my mother said, Listen, Pearl, we'll just keep it for a while. Think of it as temporary while we're living in the car. I'll get rid of it when we've got a real address with a zip code and we're safe.

I wrapped the gun up in two T-shirts and placed it in my bag.

After breakfast, Corazón said she needed to dye my hair black. We went back upstairs to the bathroom. I sat on the edge of the bathtub while Corazón stood at the sink and mixed up the hair color in a bowl with a spoon from the kitchen.

I think you'll be pretty with black hair, she said. It's only for a while. We can't have you recognized and looking strange next to me. Everyone will think I have kidnapped you.

Corazón did not stop talking as I leaned over the sink and she painted the dye into my hair with a short brush.

She said, I can't wait to see Selena's grave. It's all I can think about. To think they shot Selena and then it happened to your mother too. That boy who killed your mama had the names of the disciples of Jesus. Did you realize?

Once Corazón had dried my hair, she took my bag down to the hallway and called a taxi. We were out of the house and at the bus station just in time to catch the bus. We almost missed it. When I mentioned this to Corazón she said, Of course we almost missed it. I always almost miss the bus. It's my way.

As the taxi took us toward the bus station Corazón said, You don't look too bad with black hair. If you went home right now and walked through the trailer park no one would know it was you.

Because my mother got shot up dead, I got on a Greyhound bus. I couldn't believe it. Here I was in a vehicle looking out a window. The Greyhound bus felt just like home.

Part Three

32

Wedding dresses and shrouds come from heaven, Corazón said. You can't control when those clothes will wear you.

shroud [ʃraʊd] *Leichentuch*

I didn't pack the wedding dress, I said. I left it there. I gave it to Helen to play in.

Yes, but you're not really married.

I'm married.

Not really. One finger does not make a hand.

I know.

You realize, I let you marry him because I'm a Catholic, Corazón said. This means I don't have any judgment. I'm free.

After I'd been on the bus for twenty minutes, I got up and went to the bathroom, which was at the back behind the last row of seats. In the small compartment there was a sign in bold red letters that said WARNING: DO NOT SMOKE. Above the metal sink there was a plastic smoke detector alarm. I climbed into the sink and tore the plastic covering off the alarm and pulled out the AAA battery and threw it into the trash.

AAA *(abbr.) Bezeichnung für Mikrobatterien*

I got down from the sink, opened the window and took out a pack of cigarettes and lighter from the back pocket of my jeans. Then I lit up and blew my smoke out the window and had a good look at the highway, which was taking me farther and farther away from myself.

When I left, I threw my cigarette butt out the window. I knew I was going to be starting forest fires all across the country.

Back at my seat, Corazón said, Listen, I've been thinking. The house you were living in was beautiful.

Yes, I said.

Did you find any money lying around to steal? she asked.

No. I looked in all the drawers.

I didn't tell Corazón that Leo had given me two hundred dollars. It was all the money he'd saved up. When he gave it to me he said, Come back in one year. I'll have my inheritance by then. We'll be rich. You can have anything you want.

You smell like a cigarette, Corazón said. Were you smoking in the bathroom?

Yes, I said. Don't worry. I took the battery out of the smoke alarm.

Good girl.

We can smoke the whole way to Texas now.

I also looked around the house for money, Corazón said. I didn't find any cash either. The man must have kept some money some-

clasp *Verschluss, Schließe*

gritty *körnig*

strand *Strang*

heirloom ['eəlu:m] *Erbstück*

Laredo city on the north bank of the Rio Grande in South Texas

place. I didn't even see a safe anywhere. I did take some jewelry, though, and a watch. This is all I found in the man's bedroom.

Corazón opened her purse and took out a diamond ring, a gold wedding band, and a pearl necklace with an antique clasp.

My mother had prepared me for this day.

I placed one of the pearls against my front teeth and gently bit down and rubbed it against my teeth from side to side. The pearl was rough and slightly gritty, which meant it was real. When I held the strand in my hand the pearls were cool before they warmed in my palm, which was another test.

These are real pearls, I said. All these things you took are heirlooms. I'm sure of it. They look old. I bet they came over from Europe.

Heirloom? What's that? Corazón asked.

I knew that Mr. Brodsky would not be angry with me for stealing the jewels and running away. When he'd taken me into his home, he said he was a Jew and that Jews understood foster kids better than anyone else. You can keep the pearls because your name is Pearl, okay? I'll keep the rings and watch. Don't tell Ray about it. Ray likes us to stay in the shade so no one sees us. He says stealing stuff is standing in the sunlight.

Ray? Ray?

Do not tell Ray. No. No. He hates me stealing. He says he can buy me anything I want.

Ray? I asked again.

Yes. Ray says he can buy me anything I want, but I like to steal once in a while. Who doesn't? He just doesn't understand me. He says he loves me, but he just doesn't understand me. Men don't listen. That's a lesson for you.

Are we going to see Ray?

Yes, of course, she said. We're meeting up with Ray in Laredo. Did I forget to tell you? I guess I forgot to tell you. He called me last night. I knew he would. The most he can be away from me is three days and then he gets to feeling lost.

This was the first time Corazón had mentioned we were going to see Ray.

Corazón turned toward me.

Bend your head forward, she said. These are for you.

I leaned torward her and she placed the pearls around my neck and then carefully close the antique gold clasp.

You'll look beautiful wearing these pearls at Selena'a grave, she said.

We're going to Laredo? I asked.

Yes, after Corpus Christi, after we visit Selena.

Corazón leaned her head back on the seat and closed her eyes. Sing me a song, Pearl, she said. I've missed hearing you sing.
As the bus drove away from my fourteen years of living in a car outside a trailer park and three weeks of living in a house in foster care, I understood my legacy. My mother had not only taught me about manners and told me about her silver-spoon-cinnamon-toast childhood, she'd also given me a trust of feelings. What I only understood after she'd been killed, is she'd also had empathy for objects.
The pearls around my neck were lamenting the sea.

legacy ['legəsi] *Vermächtnis*
cinnamon *Zimt*
to lament to express sadness and feeling sorry about sth.

33

The last words Leo said to me were, How can I miss you if you don't go away?

to keep to be held onto

When he said those words my mother's voice inside me said, Pearl, sweetheart, this boy's to keep. He speaks like a song lyric.

to embroider *sticken*

I knew that those words – How can I miss you if you don't go away – were just the foster-kid motto. It could be embroidered on a pillow or printed on a T-shirt.

cusp *Spitze*

The drive took thirty-eight hours and thirty minutes and we had three transfers. The bus took us along the round northern cusp of the Gulf of Mexico. We had to go through the states of Alabama, Mississippi, and Louisiana to get from Florida to Texas.

honeymoon *Flitterwochen*

In the seats in front of us there was a married couple. I'd heard the man tell the driver they were on their honeymoon.

dull not clear
stale no longer fresh
newlyweds a newly married couple

The bride's gardenia perfume surrounded us and she was like a piece of a garden in the dull, stale air. The newlyweds brought leaves and light and land, the light, lemon-sweet land, into the bus.

From my seat I could see the tops of their heads as they moved around, leaning into each other. Sometimes, if I pressed my face close against the window, I could see them reflected in the window. They held hands, kissed, and fed each other apple slices they had in a large, square Tupperware container. Love between them was to feed the other like a mother bird. At times their conversation reached me in bits and pieces.

The husband said, You still have rice in your hair. Don't shake it out.

ache lasting pain
to track sb. down to search sb.

Thanks to my love for Leo, when I watched people love on each other, I knew I was going to give myself nothing but trouble. My ache for him was going to make me track him down again no matter what.

Acapulco city and major seaport on the Pacific coast of Mexico

On the bus, Corazón told me she'd come to the United States from Mexico ten years ago. She was from a small village in the state of Guerrero, about an hour away from Acapulco, called Eden. Ray was twenty years older than Corazón and came from Nuevo Laredo.

Hershey's kisses an American brand of chocolate, typically in the shape of teardrops
mariachi Mexican folk music dating back to the 18th century

The first time I met Ray, Corazón said, I was only a girl. I was nine years old or maybe eight. He worked with my father importing and exporting from the USA. He always brought me candy M&Ms, the yellow ones, or boxes of Hershey's kisses. I got married at age seventeen. My wedding was real. My cake was a seven-story-high cake. I had two bands play and a mariachi. We had a cockfight too. And you should know there are no divorced women in my town. There are only widows. This is the way men know they need to behave good.

I looked at Corazón's hands. Why don't you wear wedding rings? I asked.

Ay, Pearlita, you know, I flushed them down the toilet. I got so angry with Ray. I was so, so furious. I flushed those rings down the toilet.

Corazón held out her hand and touched the place where her rings should have been.

You can ask any plumber, she said. They all know that toilets are full of wedding rings.

Why doesn't Ray ever speak to me? I asked.

It's because Ray can't speak English and Ray's not going to open his mouth for people to laugh at him.

On the Greyhound bus I looked out the window at the landscape of trucks, cars, and signs. In the window's reflection I could see the pearls around my neck reflected in the pane. They were both cool and warm against my skin. Often, to my left, the blue waters of the Gulf of Mexico would shine beyond the black asphalt and trees.

pane *Fensterglass*

You know everyone is jealous of Mexico, Corazón said.

What do you mean?

Because the asteroid fell there from space. It's thanks to Mexico that there're no dinosaurs. So, you see, if it was not for Mexico, there'd be no human beings.

asteroid fell from space 66 million years ago, an asteroid hit the Earth, creating the Chicxulub crater near Yucatán and causing a global climate change and 75% of plants and animals going extinct

Twinkies brand name of an American cake snack

I reached into the pocket of my jacket and took out a pack of Twinkies. I tore open the pack with my teeth and offered one of the two yellow cakes to Corazón.

Thanks, she said, and she took one cake out of the wrapper. Where did you get the Twinkies?

wrapper *Verpackung*

I stole them from the shop at the bus station.

You steal from shops?

Well, this is almost the first time but I've been stealing cigarettes from people for ages.

Corazón said, On this trip, we're going to stop in Mobile, Alabama, to pick up some extra bags. Ray has organized this.

Mobile [moʊˈbiːl] city in southern Alabama

What for?

Don't worry about anything, Corazón said. Some man will be meeting us there. Then we'll go visit Selena's grave and, after this, we're going on to Laredo to meet up with Ray.

I broke the Twinkie in two and licked the cream filling out of the center before eating the spongy cake.

Where's Ray waiting for us?

At a hotel. We'll take a taxi from the bus station to the hotel in Laredo.

When Corazón wasn't talking to me or sleeping, she was texting to Ray on her phone. Every now and then she'd turned to me and tell me what Ray had said.

Ray says it's four duffel bags we have to pick up in Mobile, she said.

Ray says he's buying me some flowers, she said.

Ray says we shouldn't talk to any strangers, she said.

Did Ray know you came to get me? I asked.

bebé [be'be:] Spanish for baby

Of course, bebé. Ray knows everything. He knows you're just a little creature and I wasn't going to leave you behind with your mama so killed now. He lets me have anything I want. I told him you're going to be my baby.

On the bus Corazón talked about her town in Mexico. She'd never spoken about her home when we were together in her trailer. The movement of the bus made her feel she was on her way there.

As I sat beside her, taking in the faint smell of diesel and the old-air-conditioning-Greyhound-bus air, Corazón told me that her town was one hour away from the coast and from the port of Acapulco.

We don't let anybody come to our town, Corazón said. You have to have an invitation to visit. If you just drive in there, you'll get killed.

candlestick an object that holds a candle; *Kerzenhalter*

Corazón said that her town had three churches and one of them was covered in gold leaf and even had paintings that were copies of old paintings that were in Mexico City's main cathedral. The altar had candlesticks made of solid gold. In the center of the church, behind the altar, there was a copy of the painting of the Virgin of Guadalupe.

Well, Corazón said, it's supposed to be a copy. Some people say it is the real original cloth, and that the one everyone goes to visit in Mexico City's Basilica is a copy. I've been told, in secret of course, that someone in my town paid three million dollars in cash for her.

Do you think so?

In our town we know how to love God, Corazón said. So, it could be true. That Virgin of Guadalupe looks real to me.

What makes her look real?

Five armed men guard her at all times and you have to ask the priest to see her close up. He gives out the permission.

fake *Fälschung*

Then she must be real. Why would they guard a fake like that?

Okay, okay, yes, yes, she's the real one. I'm not supposed to tell.

bulletproof *kugelsicher*

She's even protected behind bulletproof glass.

34

When the bus stopped at the town of Pensacola, before leaving the state of Florida, a woman got on the bus and I understood who she was. My mother's voice said, It's happening.

I felt the woman's presence before I saw her. I felt her step on the three-step stairway leading up into the bus. Then she appeared at the end of the aisle and slowly walked toward us.

I looked at her and knew the woman fed the birds every morning. She knew when it's going to rain. Too much was expected of her. The woman was about sixty years old and very beautiful. She had dark brown eyes and gray, braided hair. The two long strands reached her waist. She probably had not cut her hair in decades. The woman was dressed in a black, long-sleeved T-shirt and a long, black skirt. She had a tattoo on her left hand, which extended out onto her fingers and disappeared under her sleeve. The inking was vines and flowers.

braided *geflochten*

inking tattoo

She sat right in the seat across from us so Corazón and the woman only had the narrow aisle between them.

When Corazón began to talk to her, I looked out the window but listened to every word.

Where are you from? Corazón asked.

The woman said she came from tideless water muck land and that she had swamp ways because she grew up in the Glades.

tideless *gezeitenlos*

Glades Everglades

She said there was a moon for everything, even for murder, and that she came from a place where all a human being needed was tobacco, coffee, sugar, salt, and matches.

Oh, well, yes, Corazón answered, and then looked down at her hands and kept quiet. She knew she'd opened the door to a crazy.

After a few minutes the woman leaned over and asked, So who's the little girl? Huh?

She's my daughter, Corazón said.

She doesn't look like she belongs to you, the woman said. What are you? A Mexican, right?

Yes, I'm Mexican, Corazón answered.

I believe you.

Don't believe me then.

I said I believe you.

Okay, Corazón said.

In Florida, the woman said, we know never to dip your feet in river water. We're a place of big rain, big wind, big thunder, big hates, she said. In Florida you need to look sharp at what you say. Be careful, predators look for the lonely, sad child.

predator sb. who follows people in order to harm them or commit a crime against them

She's safe with me, Corazón said, and placed her hand in my hand.

knots the measure of speed for ships, aircraft, etc.
velocity the speed at which an object is travelling
stardust (*lit.*) *Sternenstaub*
commotion a sudden short period of noise, confusion and excited movement
to bet on sth. *auf etw. wetten*
pasture *Weideland*
slender thin and delicate
ivy vine *Efeu*
to poke *stechen*
oracle a female priest who gave people wise but often mysterious advice from a god, or the advice given
to pat *leicht schlagen*
comfort *Trost*

Then the woman looked right at me and said, Little girl, move at the speed of knots, water velocity, not land velocity.
I listened.
She said, I want to be worthy of death. And this can only happen if we put aside the fear, the fear of the living, of living the careful life. Don't be too careful. We just happen to be stardust.
I listened.
When the bus approached Mobile, Alabama, there was a general commotion as people stood and pulled down their bags from the racks above the seats.
The woman continued to talk.
We're just stardust, the woman repeated. Have you heard of Halley's Comet? Do you know about that? It's coming back. Watch the sky. It will be here in 2061 and how old will you be then? Or will you be dead?
I'll be dead, Corazón answered. You can bet on it.
I watched the young husband and wife in the seats in front of us stand up to leave. They'd been asleep for the past couple of hours. The scent of fields and pastures and grassy hills left with them.
This is my stop, the woman said.
She stood and leaned over to Corazón to get close to me.
You, she said, and pointed her finger right at me.
Her finger was inked with a slender ivy vine that started at her nail and worked up her finger, hand, and arm.
You, she said again, and almost poked me in the face. You know the songs, don't you? I can hear them. You sure like a little fuck song, don't you?
Then the woman moved away, waved her tattooed hand at us, and walked down the aisle, off the bus, and into the city. I knew she was my goodbye-to-Florida oracle.
Who was that woman? What was that all about? Corazón asked. I really should not talk to strangers. I could be talking to the devil.
She was an Indian.
In the old days they didn't know as much about the devil as we know now, Corazón said. She smelled like vinegar.
She was a real Indian ghost, I said.
She smelled like vinegar. That's the smell of heroin. I know that smell, Corazón said.
Then she sat up straight in her seat and quickly patted both her cheeks with her hands. I couldn't tell if it was a gesture of comfort or punishment.
Or, you know, maybe it wasn't the devil or an Indian. That woman could have been an undercover cop looking for you, Corazón said. Listen to me, I could go to jail for kidnapping you out of that

foster house. There could be one of those real Amber Alerts by now. Maybe none of this was such a good idea. Ray always says my Mexican logic is too Mexican.

Nobody's looking for me. I don't even have a birth certificate.

So did your mother ever tell you, you know, who your father was?

No, she never told me. All I know is he was a schoolteacher.

Yes, that's right. He'd have gone to jail for rape, you know. Your mother was an underage girl.

I don't know.

So, you really liked that Indian woman, I could tell, Corazón said. But I figured it out in one second. She's buying and selling like everyone, practically everyone on this bus.

What do you mean?

Heroin. She was hoping I'd sell her some tar. She was trying to figure us out, but she didn't know what to think of you. I know these people. After she went to the bathroom, she was nodding. She was really gooching – that's the word.

I don't know, I said.

Well, I do know, Corazón said. In my town in Mexico, well outside the town, we grow the poppies. You walk on the hillsides covered with these wonderful red flowers and you know only one thing for sure: God forgot to give that flower a smell.

Amber Alert a child abduction emergency alert; *Informationssystem genutzt bei Vermisstmeldungen von Kindern*

underage *minderjährig*

tar (*sl.*) type of impure heroin

to nod to let your head fall forward when you are beginning to sleep

gooching (*sl.*) here: rubbing one's head between one's legs

poppy *Mohnpflanze*

35

burgundy wine-red coloured

In Mobile, Corazón and I also got off the bus with the other passengers as we had to transfer to another bus. It was a four-hour wait. We sat on the burgundy-colored metal chairs facing the bathrooms. I looked up at the ceiling fans or watched people coming in and out while Corazón bought us some Life Savers and Cokes.

Everything had been planned. Corazón and I sat in the station and, only five minutes before our bus was leaving for Corpus Christi, two men walked into the bus station. They each carried two large and very long black duffel bags.

Corazón greeted both men. I didn't recognize the Mexican, but I knew the other man because he sometimes drove the trucks that dropped off the garbage at our dump behind the trailer park. He was tall and skinny and his white skin was deeply sunburned red. He had on a short-sleeve T-shirt and I even recognized the mermaid tattoo on his right arm. I remembered seeing him talk to Ray at the dump when Ray was out looking for newspapers.

As I looked at his face I could smell the bitter rotten oranges from the dump. The man didn't recognize me with my newly dyed black hair. I wasn't going to shake up the kaleidoscope of his memory.

The two men helped Corazón get the bags and store them in the luggage compartment under the bus. We also had my duffel bag and Corazón's suitcase, which they helped to place beside the new bags.

I saw the Mexican say some words to the bus driver and give him a yellow envelope. Then the two men turned and left. They didn't even say goodbye to Corazón.

We showed our bus tickets to the conductor and got back on the bus.

Now at last I'm on my way to Selena's grave, Corazón said. This is the day I've been waiting for.

Yes.

As we moved down the highway, Corazón was a jukebox of Selena's songs.

I leaned against the window and looked out.

As soon as I began to feel a little drowsy the guns were there. My empathy malady for objects was blooming as we moved down the highway above hundreds of crimes.

In the belly of the Greyhound bus there was a Smith & Wesson M&P assault rifle, DPMS Panther Arms assault rifle, Smith & Wesson handgun, Llama handgun, Glock pistol, Smith & Wesson pistol, Taurus pistol, Del-Ton assault rifle, .40-caliber semiautomatic pistol, .45-caliber Glock, Beretta pistol, Smith & Wesson semiautomatic pistol, Remington shotgun, Bushmaster XM-15 rifle, .22-caliber Savage Mark II rifle, Springfield Armory semiautomatic handgun, Smith & Wesson semiautomatic rifle, Remington shotgun, Glock .40-caliber semiautomatic pistol, FN Herstal pistol, Beretta 92 FS 9mm pistol, and a Beretta PX4 Storm pistol.

I could feel the guns under me and their presence entered the bus along with the vehicle's exhaust fumes. Back at the trailer, I'd watched Corazón clean them and I'd most likely helped her tag almost every one.

And I could hear the song like an anthem: *I have a hard time missing you baby, with my pistol in your mouth. Just roll your pretty eyes if you intend to stay.*

There was a day when a deer, a white-tailed deer, made the mistake of wandering into our trailer park. When April May and I came home from school, the dead deer was lying on the ground, right in front of her trailer. Blood oozed out of its body. The mammal lay on its side and its eyes were closed. It was pockmarked with dozens of holes. April May's father had killed the animal.

It only came to visit, April May said. It would have left in a little while.

She said this with sadness. In our world of reptiles and amphibians the doe held too much beauty to be on our land.

Ride it, girls, ride that deer, Sergeant Bob said to us when we stood looking at the carcass.

I want to take a photograph of you riding that thing. Look at its size. It's big. Man, that's a big deer.

It was a humid day. The air was a stew of mosquitoes. Flies were already buzzing around the dead animal. It smelled bad.

April May's father was wearing his army combat uniform and stood on two legs, which meant he'd attached his prosthetic to his stump. He was still holding the shotgun in one hand.

I could see that Noelle, who rarely left her trailer, was standing behind a tree, watching everything.

Later, when I asked Noelle what she thought about Sergeant Bob killing the deer, she said, Don't worry. No one will mourn.

And no one came over to look. Pastor Rex, Mrs. Roberta Young, the Mexicans, and my mother never showed up. Even Rose stayed inside the trailer hoping it would all be over soon. The fact that no one came out of their trailers to see what was going on had more to do with April May's father than the animal. There wasn't a person who didn't know that April May's father could become unhinged.

Come on, girls, ride that deer. Come on, girls, giddap, April May's father insisted.

to ooze to flow slowly out of sth.
mammal *Säugetier*

doe the female of animals such as deer or rabbits

carcass the body of a dead animal

stew *Eintopf*; here: the air was thick with mosquitoes

to mourn *trauern*

unhinged mentally ill

giddap (*coll.*) get up

We didn't want to get near the carcass and flies.

We backed away.

No, April May answered. It's not a horse even.

clumsy *schwerfällig*

Her father dropped the shotgun and in two long, clumsy strides he was at April May's side. He wrapped his hand around her upper arm, which lay in his hand as slim as a plastic drinking straw, and pulled her over to the deer and shoved her down on its belly.

to smear sth. to spread sth. sticky over sth.

By this time April May was crying. She was wearing shorts and I could see that her bare legs were getting smeared with the animal's blood. I'd never seen her cry.

I felt bad for April May but not bad enough, and so I ran home to my car as fast as I could. I locked myself in the Mercury and lay down flat on the backseat under my mother's pile of plastic bags.

The next day April May and I walked back from school together.

I knew she wasn't going to be angry. In Florida no one blames anyone for running away from anything.

What happened to the deer? I asked her.

to drag sth. to move sth. by pulling it along the surface

He dragged it into the dump and left it there.

We better stay away from there for some time.

You bet, April May answered.

Ezekiel phrophet in the Hebrew Bible

The following Sunday at church Pastor Rex said that this was the day for Ezekiel. It made me think of the deer as if the animal deserved a prayer.

Prophesy to the breath prophesy by Ezekiel in the Old Testament
mortal *der/die Sterbliche*
to slay (slew, slain) to kill in a violent way

Pastor Rex read, Prophesy to the breath, prophesy, mortal, and say to the breath: Thus says the Lord God: Come from the four winds, O breath, and breathe upon these slain, that they may live.

bucket *Eimer*

And once I knew we had four bags of guns in the bus, I knew my old life would be over. I'd never erase the blackboard of my mind or wash away my memory like it was a bucket full of dirt.

substitute *Ersatz*

Thanks to my mother I knew memory was the only substitute for love. Thanks to my mother I knew the dream world was the only place to go.

My mother always said, Dreaming is cheap. It doesn't cost a thing. In dreams you don't have to pay the bills or pay the rent. In dreams you can buy a house and be loved back.

In the Greyhound bus I remembered another day at the trailer park. This was shortly after my forever-and-ever fight with April May, and I still did not know we would never speak to each other again. Now it seemed so stupid that we were no longer friends.

On the day that came back to me in the bus, it had been raining.

The hurricane that had been forecast had missed Florida and had weakened over the Gulf of Mexico. There had not been a storm, but there had been a weekend of clouds.

On that afternoon, Eli was in the Mercury with my mother and I was at Corazón and Ray's trailer doing my homework.

Corazón was cleaning a gun on the kitchen counter.

On that day, as the rain fell nonstop on the metallic roof of the trailer, Corazón gasped and threw the gun she was cleaning back on the countertop.

to gasp *keuchen*

What am I looking at? Corazón asked.

The weapon skidded off the stainless-steel surface and fell on the floor.

to skid off to slide off; *heraus-rutschen*

What's the matter?

Corazón took a few steps away from the gun and covered her mouth with one hand.

Look! She said and pointed at the gun.

What is it?

Oh, oh, she said.

What's wrong?

This gun. Look, she still has blood all over her.

I stood up and walked over to Corazón's side and looked down at the gun on the floor.

The weapon was dark brown, and we both knew we were looking at old, dried blood.

What're you going to do? I asked.

What do you think I'm going to do?

Call the police?

No, Corazón said. No. Get out the Tide.

This gun was on the Greyhound bus.

36

to doze off to be half asleep

If you want to find out who loves you, just get sick, Corazón said. We'd both dozed off after leaving Mobile, and Corazón shook me awake with these words.

If you want to find out who loves you, just get sick, she said again.

What made you think of that?

It's just my own grandmother's advice. I remembered it right now and I wanted to tell you before I forget. So what do you think this means?

I don't know, I said.

It means you have to fake being sick all the time so that you know who loves you! Okay?

Okay, I answered.

There's one thing I've never been able to figure out, Corazón said.

What is it?

disarranged confused

What can you do when you have a crazy desire for a married man? You can't sleep. You're disarranged.

Does this happen to you? I asked.

Ay, my Pearlita, she said. You're still so young.

from sea to shining sea verse taken from *America the Beautiful*, a patriotic American song; here: reference to the buses travelling all over the country
germ *Keim, Bakterie*
to cringe *erschaudern*
to peer to look carefully
filth thick, unpleasant dirt

At the beginning of the trip I used to go into the bathroom and try not to touch any of the from-sea-to-shining-sea Greyhound germs I knew were all over the place. It made me cringe to think of all these people who'd been in there. In the open garbage I could peer in and see a baby's diaper, an old syringe, and a book. I didn't dare reach my hand in there and see what the book was about. Boredom was not enough for me to make peace with the filth.

Corazón obviously didn't share my feelings as she came back after several trips to the bathroom and said, Hey, I was reading that book in the trash. It was about fly-fishing. Did you know people make their flies? It's complicated. They have to tie knots and make them look like insects in order to trick the fish.

I had no idea.

Look at it next time you go to the bathroom, Corazón said.

As we moved closer to Texas, Corazón talked about Selena and her town in Mexico.

fifteenth birthday party Quinceañera celebration marking the transition from childhood to adulthood in South American countries
Christina Aguilera (*1980) American singer and song-writer whose father is from Ecuador
Jennifer Lopez (*1969) American singer and actress of Puerto-Rican descent

We have the best parties, she said. The best music. One of my nieces wanted to have a famous singer sing at her fifteenth birthday party. And her father brought her one of those famous ones, you know. Christina Aguilera or Jennifer Lopez. One of those. A Latina. I can't remember who it was, because I was here, in the United States, when they had that party. On December twelfth for the Virgin of Guadalupe Day another uncle of mine covers the whole town in roses in vases and buckets. Everyone in that area of Mexico knows there isn't a single rose to be bought; he gets them all.

As the hours passed and we moved closer to Corpus Christi, Corazón stopped talking about her childhood and became very excited and began to hum Selena's song 'Tu Solo Tu.'

She'd organized everything. We were going to stay at the hotel were Selena had been shot and killed. Corazón knew, through the Selena Fan Club, that the room number where Selena had been shot as she ran away from the bullets had been changed from 158 to 150.

The hotel does not charge extra for the room, Corazón said. I think all they ever did was change the carpet. When I called to make a reservation they acted like they didn't know what I was talking about.

carpet *Teppich(boden)*

Are we staying in that room, I asked.

You know, I thought about it, Corazón said. But I changed my mind. I think if I stayed in that room, I'd get so terribly sad I'd just be sad for the rest of my life. I'd never be able to rub it off.

The city of Corpus Christi was built on the edge of Corpus Christi Bay. As we drove in we could see rows of sailboats lined up tied to the docks. The sky was a light blue and the bay water was a deep black blue. Between these two blue tunnels of sky and water we drove into the Greyhound bus station.

Before we got off the bus, Corazón whispered to me, We're not taking those bags with us. Just get your own bag and I'll get mine. Ray has arranged for someone to pick them up and get them to Laredo.

I was very happy to get away from those guns that gave me the let's-not-forget-what-we-killed dreams.

We took a taxi to the hotel.

It's 901 Navigation Boulevard, Corazón said to the taxi driver. She said the words slowly, as if saying the address were like reading a poem.

Corazón rolled down the window and looked at the city. This day could be March 31, 1995, she said. It feels like that day.

We checked in at the lobby where Selena had run up for help with a bullet wound in her shoulder. Corazón gave the hotel clerk her charge card and then looked around the lobby as the clerk activated our key cards.

Nothing has changed, Corazón said.

We walked toward our room and over the ground where Selena had fallen. Corazón walked lightly on tiptoe over the tiles, as if she might crush something. She also spoke softly, as if she didn't want to wake someone up.

funeral home *Bestattungsunternehmen*
mesquite tree small trees native to Mexico and southwestern USA
wrought-iron *schmiedeeisern*
tomb [tu:m] *Grabmal*
hollow-point bullet *Hohlspitzgeschoss*
in the wake and tide (*lit.*) sth. happening after and because of sth.
grove a group of sth. standing close to each other
to wait up to not go to bed at night because you are expecting sb. to arrive
to catch up (*phr. v.*) to reach sb./sth. by moving faster than the other person or thing
devotion loyalty, love or care for sb./sth.

That night, after we ate a pizza we'd ordered in, we lay side by side in two twin beds. I expected she'd be talking to me all night, but as soon as she got under the covers she said, This hotel is like a temple.

She never said another word.

The next morning Corazón and I went to Selena's grave.

A taxi took us to Seaside Memorial Park and Funeral Home. The taxi driver knew exactly where we were going.

Everyone from out of town here comes to see Selena, he said. He spoke English with a strong Mexican accent.

Everybody loved her, he said. Once I even brought two transvestites from Mexico City to visit her and they were crying the whole time.

I'm going to cry too, Corazón said. That's what tears are for.

It was a large cemetery, with small graves except for Selena's, which was a small monument and really stood out in the flat landscape. Under the largest mesquite tree in the cemetery, her grave was surrounded by a wrought-iron gate and signs that stated: STAY OUT. RESPECT THE GRAVE SITE.

On the tomb was the image of Selena's face engraved in bronze. At the base of the sculpture was written: Selena Quintanilla-Perez: April 16, 1971 – March 31, 1995.

Now I see her grave, Corazón said. I believe it. Selena's dead.

Corazón bowed her head and looked at the quote that was carved at the base. She read the words aloud, He will actually swallow up death forever, and the Sovereign Lord Jehovah will certainly wipe the tears from all faces. Isaiah.

I walked around the grave and stood under the encircling shade of the tree.

She's an angel, Corazón said. How could someone kill her?

I didn't want to look at Corazón's face. I knew that she was crying and didn't want to comfort her.

There was a breeze that stirred in the sky of branches above me. I felt drowsy and could see it all.

On that day of days Selena ran away from the gun with a .38-caliber hollow-point bullet in her body. In the wake and tide of her escape she left a 392-foot-long trail of blood.

Selena was a black sparrow lifting her wings and she bled out as she ran across the field of the parking lot, through the grove of cars, toward the long grass of the hotel lobby. She was calling. Wait wait wait for me. She was calling for death to wait up, she was catching up, she was almost there.

I have devotion, Corazón said. She was walking around the grave looking at the fan letters, which were propped against or stuck on the iron fence with tape that circled the site. I have devotion just like these people, Corazón continued. I should have brought a letter too. We should have brought flowers.

Some of the fan letters were in sealed envelopes. Nobody would ever read them.

When I stand here, I think that every time I look at a grave it makes me miss the people before my time, Corazón said. Do you miss the people you never knew?

Yes, I said. I never knew anyone.

We spent a few more minutes at Selena's grave and then walked through the cemetery and back to the road, where the taxi driver had waited for us.

Corazón asked him to drive us downtown to the Municipal Marina.

municipal marina *städt. Hafenanlage*

The taxi driver was in a talkative mood. It's my great privilege to bring you to Selena's grave, he said. I always say that I bring people here and it's my way to keep Selena alive.

If April May had been with us, she'd have said, Man this man knows how to get a good tip!

tip *Trinkgeld*

Corazón gave the taxi driver an extra five dollars when we got out of the taxi.

Let's go to the water, Corazón said.

We walked down one dock, past tall sailboats and motorboats, to the very end of the long walkway. There we sat down cross-legged on the wood planks and looked out at the bay.

The blue-black water reminded me of afternoons after school when April May and I would go smoke at the river. She was the only person who knew who I was. She knew to dare me to take off my shoes and sink my feet in the alligator-infested waters. If I'd lived under a roof, she would have dared me to jump off it.

Once she dared me to drink a beer when I was only nine years old because she said it would make me tell the truth. I did get drunk and she asked me all kinds of questions. She'd drawn up a list, which included asking me who my father was and if I was capable of killing.

April May did not dare me to cross the highway with my eyes closed. She knew I'd do it.

At the Municipal Marina dock looking out at the bay, Corazón and I sat close together so that my upper arms rubbed against hers. It made me think about how we accidently touch other people's bodies and then always say we're sorry. I was not sorry. I moved even closer, leaned into her, so that our knees also touched.

If it hadn't been for my life, I know I would have been somebody, Corazón said. But I can't get away from my life because it's my life.

to unfurl *entfalten*
to billow to bulge as a sail in the wind; *blähen, bauschen*
to sway to move slowly from side to side
nugget-size small lump like a gold nugget
drawn and quartered medieval punishment; *gestreckt und gevierteilt*

In the distance a sailboat unfurled a sail and it blew open like a billowing wedding dress.

On the dock next to us two boys were flying red and blue kites.

I could hear the sound of the wind all around me as it moved everything and made the world sway and shake.

The gun was at the bottom of the bay.

On Monday, June 10, 2002, the five-shot, wooden-handled .38-caliber Taurus revolver used to kill Selena was cut into fifty nugget-size pieces with a saw and dumped into Corpus Christi Bay. It was Jose Longoria, a Texas district court judge, who ordered the weapon destroyed and thrown into the bay.

If April May had been here beside me she would have said, That idiot judge had the gun drawn and quartered.

I looked out over the Body-of-Christ-water gun grave,

I knew that even though April May had given me the alcohol truth-serum lie detector test, I still had no idea who I was.

37

Afterward. I had not thought about afterward. I had not thought about what was going to happen after the visit to Selena's grave. Corazón was just sweeping me along into her life. She was the broom and I was dust.

I was that kid who isn't thinking and drives too fast and drinks too much. I was just living inside the word 'risk' as if it were an address.

On the bus on our way to Laredo to meet with Ray, I thought about Leo and wished I were back in Mr. Brodsky's clean house.

I was beginning to think that I needed to make a U-turn. This made me think of my mother and I remembered our pretend drives when she said, Okay, let's go on a road trip. Leave skid marks. Go over the speed limit. Let's go backward. Make a U-turn. Backward.

On the Greyhound bus, driving toward Laredo and Ray, I only wanted to go backward. I wanted my car living, my powdered-milk-mixed-with-water-milk, the smell of Raid on my skin, and the taste of sugar cubes dissolving on my tongue.

All that was left of my old life was a Jesus-on-the-cross plastic toothbrush lying on the riverbed of bullets.

I asked Corazón if she had a little bag of sugar. She was always stealing packets of sugar and tea bags. Her purse was full of everything she could pick along the way.

I wanted some sugar, but Corazón had only a yellow packet of Splenda. It was better than nothing. I ripped it open and poured the powder into my hand and licked it off my palm. Many things are better than nothing.

I've never known anyone to eat Splenda raw like that, Corazón said.

I haven't either.

What happened was, after the excitement of visiting Selena's grave, all I could think about was my mother and Leo.

Corazón watched as the walking-the-train-track sadness took me over.

to sweep (swept, swept) sb. along to move sb., esp. quickly and powerfully

to dissolve *sich auflösen*

purse (*US*) a handbag

Splenda brand name of an artificial sweetener; *Süßstoff*

raw here: on its own

38

The River Inn hotel in Laredo was close to the Rio Grande and the Mexico and United States border. The place was run-down. The plants in the pots were dead and the tile floor of the lobby was cracked. The swimming pool was empty but had a few old plastic balls in it. Kids must go down the metal ladder, I thought, and play ball in that waterless hole.

tile *Kachel, Fliese*

The hotel was built on the side of the highway, so the sound of trucks driving past never stopped.

The woman at the reception knew Corazón well and greeted her in a mixture of Spanish and English. She explained that Ray had already checked in and had even requested an additional room for me.

to request sth. to ask for sth. politely or officially

Ray likes this place because it's always empty. No one ever stays here, Corazón said as we walked toward the rooms, which were lined up in a row facing the parking lot. Our rooms were side by side.

See you soon, Corazón said. Unpack. Take a shower.

Corazón was breathless. I knew that excitement. I'd seen it in my mother. I'd felt it when I knew Leo was about to come home from school. Her eyes were looking for Ray. She knew he was close by.

My hotel room smelled like a lavender-and-vanilla-scented Mr. Clean. I knew the smell well, as my mother used to steal bottles of the cleaning liquid from the VA hospital. She used it to scrub the inside of our Mercury because we were always fighting the mold, which grew easily on the car's upholstery and rugs in Florida's wet air. The smell of Mr. Clean stuck around our car for days.

scent a pleasant natural smell

mold *Schimmel*

upholstery *Polsterstoff*

I placed my bag on the bed and unzipped it. The first thing I did was take out Eli's small black gun, which was wrapped inside my T-shirts. I looked around the room for a place to hide it, and placed it under the pillow on the bed.

I was even beginning to think that maybe I should have left the gun in the Mercury along with the bag of Domino sugar cubes and the box of Cheerios.

On the drive to Laredo, Corazón had warned me that the hotel was pretty awful, but when you've lived in a car any hotel is a palace, even if there were cockroaches and stains on the sheets and old rugs.

cockroach *Kakerlake*
stain *Fleck*
rug *Teppich*

I really wanted to take a long, hot shower, but I wanted a cigarette even more. Corazón had the cigarettes, so I went out to find her and get some before bathing.

I knocked and Corazón did not open. She asked who it was from the other side of the closed door.

It's me. It's Pearl, I said. Me.

What do you want? she asked.

The door was still closed.

Corazón opened the door a crack. Just a minute, she said, and she walked back into the room, leaving me at the door.

I pushed the door a little and peered in.

The room had two queen-sized beds in it.

The four duffel bags we'd picked up in Mobile and transported on the bus were laying zipped open on one of the beds. On the other bed, the guns were laid out by size as if they were being counted. There were crumpled and folded newspapers, which looked like old wrapping paper at a birthday party, everywhere. The newspapers had been used to package the guns.

Corazón took the cigarettes out of her bag and turned and saw me standing in the doorway looking into the room.

Oh, what the hell, come in and smoke with me, Corazón said. There's no place to sit down. What am I supposed to do with my suitcase? What am I supposed to do with my things? Ray's taken over this whole room with the guns!

Corazón's suitcase was still unopened by the bathroom door.

You can see Ray's counting them up. He doesn't trust anybody. Then he has to wrap them all again. And he's right. The truth is, Pastor Rex is always saying there's fifty guns when there's forty-eight, like that. He's always cheating. You know.

These are Pastor Rex's guns?

Yes, of course, Corazón said. Yes.

So, Eli's here?

Yes, of course.

Is Pastor Rex here too?

No. No. He and Eli had a big fight. We have not heard from Señor Rex because he said that your mother being killed ruined the business for all of us. Yes, the police found out about the guns and we all had to get out of there. I had to leave everything behind.

I knew that Pastor Rex's trailer and Corazón and Ray's trailer were going to sit there empty for years. Abandoned homes in trailer parks were everywhere – all across the United States of America. I also knew that April May would never have the guts to explore Pastor Rex's left-behind stuff without me.

So Eli's here? I'm going to see him? I asked. His name tolled inside of me.

Yes. Of course.

And the song came. And the song was in my head. The song was singing and it was Louisiana Red: *You're tied to me girl I can feel your sweetblood call even if you sneak away I'll find you before nightfall 'cause you are tied to me girl I can feel your sweetblood call.*

And I heard my mother, with words like after-a-prayer amens, she said, Bad luck is better than no luck at all.

queen-sized *überdurchschnittlich groß*

to have the guts to be brave; to have the courage

to toll to sound as a large bell does

Louisiana Red (1932 – 2012) African-American blues guitarist and singer

39

SUV (*abbr.*) Sports Utility Vehicle

to truck sth. in to transport sth. somewhere in a truck

to require to demand
ancestry *Vorfahren*

matrilineal *in der Erbfolge der mütterlichen Linie folgend*
kinship *Verwandtschaft*

Putnam County a county located in the northeast of Florida

whooping crane *Schreikranich*

Daytona Beach a city in the northeast of Florida, famous for its 37km-long beach which can be cruised with motorized vehicles
sibling *Bruder oder Schwester*

You can help me pack up these guns. Ray's counted them and has gone off to take care of some things and get the SUV we keep parked in a garage. If you help me, it will go faster. All I want is a shower after those long hours on that dog bus.

I walked on the crumpled newspapers as I entered the room. I pushed the empty duffel bags to one side so I could sit on the edge of the bed while I helped Corazón wrap up the guns again. A strong scent of vinegar lifted up out of the canvas bags.

I looked at the newspapers around me and I could see Ray looking for newspapers at the dump of my trailer park and buying newspapers from the men who trucked in the garbage. The piles of newspapers outside Corazón and Ray's trailer appeared before my eyes. On rainy days, Corazón would cut open large plastic garbage bags and run outside and cover up the papers so they would not get wet.

I looked at the newspapers filling up a room of the River Inn. I looked at the guns piled up on one bed.

There was no song inside me.

Help me, Corazón said. We can do this quickly.

I picked up a rifle. It had a tag on it written in my handwriting.

As I wrapped up a DPMS Panther Arms assault rifle, I looked over the newspaper I was wrapping it in. I read, The Florida Miccosukee Indians require members to have at least half-Miccosukee ancestry, and will accept individuals with Miccosukee mothers who are not enrolled in any other tribe. They are a matrilineal system of kinship and inheritance. Children are born into their mother's clan, from which they gain their status in the tribe.

As I wrapped up a Smith & Wesson M&P assault rifle, I read, Following a call to a fire in the woods, Putnam County Sheriff's Office deputies followed a trail to a one-pot meth operation in a shed, a Sheriff's Office report stated.

As I wrapped up a .22-caliber Savage Mark II rifle, I read, The annual winter migration of endangered whooping cranes to Florida has been completed with the help of ultralight aircraft.

As I wrapped a Del-Ton assault rifle, I read, A Florida judge will consider a deal for a mother who drove her kids into the ocean in her minivan during a hearing in Daytona Beach. That same morning, police arrested a central Florida father two weeks after his 5-year-old son shot his 2-year-old sibling. Also, that same morning, a mother of three was arrested Thursday after one of her children was found walking alone on a major highway. The 12-year-old youngster was carrying a luggage bag and a backpack. She was trying to run away. Authorities said the child was unable to provide a home address.

As I folded, I read, Over one diamond, the singleton is not good news; North should quietly bid one heart, four-card suits up the bidding ladder.

As I placed the guns one on top of another in piles by size, I read the horoscope sections. Under Taurus, I read, Sometimes your favorite things are not your favorite things. Under Virgo I read, Travel and romance are encouraged.

I wrapped up three .223-caliber AR-15 rifles, a Beretta PX4 Storm pistol, a Glock pistol, a Smith & Wesson pistol, a Taurus pistol, a .40-caliber semiautomatic pistol, a .45-caliber Glock, a Beretta pistol, two Smith & Wesson semiautomatic pistols, a Remington shotgun, and a Bushmaster XM-15 rifle and read the comics, the classifieds, the sports, the weather, the TV guide, and birth announcements.

I read all the obituaries.

diamond a playing card, *Karo*
singleton *Bridge: mit nur einer Karte in einer Spielfarbe*
to bid *ein Gebot machen, reizen*
to suit up (*phr. v.*) weiter reizen können
bidding ladder *Abfolge der Gebote*
Taurus *Sternzeichen des Stiers*
Virgo *Sternzeichen der Jungfrau*

classifieds *Kleinanzeigen*

obituary [əˈbɪtʃʊəri] *Traueranzeige*

40

Late that night there was a soft knock on my door.
I didn't get up to answer and called out, Come in.
I was sure it was Corazón coming to get her Bic lighter I'd run off with.
The door opened.
I heard his voice before I saw him.
What are you doing here, girl?
Eli stood at the door. The light from the parking lot behind him created a silhouette of his body and the hat on his head kept his face in shadow. Eli wore a hat even if it was the middle of the night. In Eli's world the moon burned hotter than the sun.
I sat up in my bed and pulled the covers close to my chest.
He was wearing Mr. Don't Come Back's silver cowboy belt with the gold eagle flying, rounded wings open, in the center of the buckle.
The next thing Eli said to me in his song-voice was, Oh sweet sweet sweet lovely, what have you done to your hair?
Dyed it.
Why? Are you in a beauty show? You running?
Maybe.
Did Corazón steal you or did you come away with her?
Maybe.
He said, Is that the only word you know? The word 'maybe'?
Maybe, I said.
You owe her money I bet. Where'd you get that noose of pearls that's around your neck?
Is everything for you about owing?
I was saying. I'm not accusing.
Eli closed the door of my room behind him and walked toward me. He moved slowly with one boot in front of the other.
I was chewing on my hate for him.
The eagle was swooping through tall grass and soaring up into the blue night sky toward the telephone wires.
Outside I could hear voices in the parking lot. I knew the Indian ghosts were there. I could hear them whisper as they walked the Trail of Tears. It was a whisper that sounded like, *Safety, safety, safety, the Great Brilliance is beginning.*
The only time I'd ever been alone with Eli was when I'd seen him for the first time sitting naked on a bed in Pastor Rex's trailer with a shotgun across his knees.
Eli was only two steps away from my bed.
I said, Stop there.
Hush, hush, shh. Hush, he said. We both need a shoulder.

chest *Brust*
to run here: to take part
to owe sth. to sb. *jdm. etw. schulden*
noose *Schlinge*
to swoop (*infml.*) to make a sudden attack on a place or group of people in order to surround and catch them
to soar up to rise very quickly to a high level
wire *Kabel*
Trail of Tears (1831 – 1850) the forced relocation of Native Americans from their homelands to reservations in southwestern areas of the USA; people were forced to march to the reservations

Get out.

Listen, Pearl, Eli said. I miss Margot too. She went to heaven.

When he said Margot I heard my mother's name inside his body where he kept it hidden after he'd stolen it like money, stolen it like a Bible out of a hotel room.

Sure you miss her. Sure you do, I said. I bet you miss her all the time. You didn't even take your hat off for my killed mother's daughter.

Eli took off his hat and placed it on the bed.

You're a liar, I said.

Ah. The thief calls me a liar?

I reached for the gun that was under my pillow and held it out toward him.

Eli looked at the gun and stopped walking toward me.

Don't come close, I said.

Hey, hey, hey. Pearl, what're you doing?

Remember, you gave us this gun, Mr. Eli, I said. Do you remember? You told my mother it was for our safety.

I did want you to be safe. It seemed no good for a young woman and girl to be living in a car without a gun. Put it down.

Say your last words, I said. What're your last words going to be?

Please. Hey, Pearl, put that gun down. Stop it.

What are you doing in my room? Why did you come here? It's late.

I just wanted you to know I'm your friend. I want to comfort you. Also, if you put down that gun I'll tell you who your father was. Your sweet mama never told you. I know this. Margot told me you didn't know.

I don't believe you, Mr. Eli.

She didn't want you to think you could go looking for him. Your mama didn't want you to be poking around with a stick and stirring everything up.

I knew I wanted to shoot him dead. He was just a truth-tricker with a sharp tack in his shoe.

to poke around here: to investigate sth.
to stir sth. up (*phr. v.*) to cause a problem to grow
tack *Reißzwecke*

Put down the gun, Eli said. Pearl, little oyster-shell girl, put down that gun. I'll tell you. Listen. Your daddy was that piano player, you know, the man who gave your mother piano lessons.

Stop lying. You live with your fingers crossed behind our back.

That piano player liked to suck on sugar cubes.

I held my breath and tightly gripped the gun my mother had taught me to use down at our river.

Your father always carried sugar cubes in his pockets.

Eli wasn't lying.

My mother played the piano across the dashboard of the car and I didn't even know it was my father she was playing for.

tonic *Tonika; Grundton einer Tonleiter*
sharps *Erhöhungszeichen*
rests *Pausen*
semitone *Halbton*
interval *Tonhöhenabstand*
legato *gebundene Tonfolge*
chord *Akkord*
arpeggio *Art von Akkord*

daredevil *Draufgänger*

mercy *Gnade*
lost-and-found box a place where *lost items* are kept till they are collected by their owners

divine intervention when God reaches down and saves sb. from a dangerous situation
chorus *Chor*

I was born from the tonic, flats, sharps, rests, born from tones, semitones and intervals, born from legatos, chords, and arpeggios and metronome-heart beating: love, love, love, love, love, love, love, love.

But Eli should have known better. He could sweet-talk a grown-up woman, but he couldn't sweet-talk this girl he'd just gifted a father. Eli Redmond didn't know he had spoken his honey words to a champion, gold-medal daredevil.

I had no feelings for him.

He had no broken bones.

In that room the word 'mercy' was in the lost-and-found box.

I looked down at my hand and at my father's blue opal ring on my finger.

Eli should've known nothing good ever happens after midnight.

I looked up at Eli. I pointed the gun. I shot him. I shot him for my mother and with the divine intervention of her chorus of singers singing the blues.

41

Cleaning fingerprints off of everything in a hotel room is a true act of kindness.

Corazón heard the shot that killed Eli and came to my room.

Pearl, are you in there? she asked, and knocked on the door.

I didn't answer.

Corazón opened the door.

I was still sitting in my bed, under the covers. Eli was lying on the floor. I had not missed.

Corazón took care of everything. She wiped my fingerprints off all the surfaces while I sat in the bed and Eli lay on the hotel-room rug dying over and over again. Every time I looked down to where he lay, he died again as if looking were shooting.

Corazón took care of everything as if she were cleaning up popped balloons and paper plates covered with chocolate icing left over from a birthday party. She was bringing down the streamers and sweeping up confetti.

icing *Glasur*

streamer *Luftschlange*

When she'd finished, Corazón helped to dress me as if I were six years old. She buttoned up my blouse, held my jeans while I stepped into them, and then zipped them up. She knelt on the rug and tied my sneakers.

She packed up all my things.

Then she picked up my gun that was lying on the bed and placed it in the front left pocket of her jeans.

I knew I would love her for the rest of my life because she wasn't angry. She didn't scold me.

to scold sb. *jdn. ausschimpfen*

Then Corazón took me to her room and gave me a glass of water.

Listen, Corazón said, we're going to Mexico. As soon as Ray gets here in the morning with the car we'll cross the border. We need to get out here first thing. In my town you'll be almost the whitest person anyone has ever seen. They've seen blondes, but nothing so strange like you except for a donkey that was once born an albino. Someone once saw a white dolphin in Acapulco. That was even in the newspapers.

I knew my mother would say, what has happened to you was not in the Lamb's Book of Life.

As far as I could tell, no one in my family was in that book.

Corazón explained to me that the men who worked for Ray – the ones who'd taken the bags of guns in Mobile – would be dealing with Eli's body.

You don't have to worry about a thing, she said. Ray is that kind of man who takes care of everything.

In Corazón's hotel room, she took a leftover newspaper out of the trash and used it to wrap up my revenge-maker gun. Then she unzipped the duffel bag assigned to the handguns and placed it inside.

This gun, she has to go with the other guns, Corazón said.

Is Ray going to be angry? I asked.

Of course not, Corazón said. There's no man on Earth who liked Eli Redmond.

When I listened to my heart, I heard footsteps.

All night long I sat in the hotel room smoking cigarettes one after another.

The way long night we both knew smoking was keeping us alive.

way (*adv.*, *infml.*) far too

42

When Ray arrived in the morning, Corazón and I were still sitting in the room wakeful to our Eli vigil. Two message-in-a-bottle plastic water bottles filled with cigarette butts were on the bedside table.

vigil *Nachtwache*

When Ray walked in, he found us in a closed room thick with smoke and surrounded by the bags stuffed with guns.

I stood and slipped out of the room. I didn't want to hear Corazón tell Ray what had happened and listen to my life in words.

I stepped out of the hotel room into the cool, new morning air and didn't look next door, toward the room-horizon where Eli lay.

One after another the trucks and cars drove down the highways. I tasted the mix of diesel and exhaust fumes. A light spray of dew covered the gray cement ground of the hotel's parking lot.

dew *Tau*

I looked up. On that day of days the moon was still in the sky because that night was not going away so fast. It was sticking around for the last scraps.

scrap small amount of sth.

After a few minutes Ray and Corazón came outside. Each of them was carrying one of the heavy bags filled with guns.

Ray brushed past and walked straight toward the car. Of course I knew he'd never speak a word.

Corazón stopped next to me and placed the bag down on the ground.

Don't worry, she said. I told you Ray wouldn't be angry. He only said it was better late than never, which means he wishes it had happened sooner. You know, Ray does not give that much importance to life. He says you swatted a fly.

to swat sth. to hit sth., esp. an insect, with a flat object

I walked over to the car with Corazón. Ray placed two of the long bags in the trunk and then lay another down across the backseat. Ray looked at me and pointed at the car.

I understood.

Corazón held open the car door and got inside. I lay down across the backseat on top of a bag of guns. At first it was uncomfortable but then I moved around until I found a spot where the metal settled beneath me. I lay on my back so I could see out the rear window.

My body was as long as a hunting rifle.

Then Corazón placed another bag, the one containing pistols, lightly on top of my body.

The bag above me also settled and I could feel the weight of dozens of pistols wrapped in newspapers through the canvas. Eli's gun was in good company.

You'll be hidden like this, Corazón said. No one can look in and see you.

I was home. I'd been lying across the backseat of a car my whole life. I was in my mother's bedroom.

Corazón explained that every month they paid a border guard to let them bring the guns into Mexico, but that taking a child might create problems.

Once we cross over, you can come and sit in the front seat with me, she said. This won't take too much time. Just take it easy. Let's hope there's not too much traffic. Once we get across the bridge, everything will be fine.

Ray turned on the engine, backed up, and then slowly drove the car away from the hotel, away from the body of Eli Redmond, away and away and toward the border.

Corazón could not stop talking. She was filling up my silence with her words.

You'll see, she said, Mexico is the most beautiful country in the world. It's true. You will love her. Everyone speaks Spanish. We know there is speech in silence. We know you can love someone and never tell them. You'll never want to leave. Maybe you'll be famous and sing at parties. I'll show you everything and it will not be a dream.

From my space under the bags there was still a tiny crack through which I could look up at the sky through the back window.

It's going to rain, Corazón said. Look at those black clouds.

A few drops began to fall.

I thought of Leo in the foster home sleeping in my my-love-for-my-killed-mother tears.

We're crossing now, Corazón said.

I knew I'd be coming back to the United States someday for Leo and to look up my father in the Yellow Pages of life.

We're on the bridge, Corazón said. It's the Juárez-Lincoln Bridge. We're going over the river.

I looked up at the sky and took in my first breath that belonged to no country.

Outside, a few larger drops of rain began to fall and break on the glass pane and then it slowly began to rain, rain and morning thunder, and so the windows were bleeding down water.

The morning became as dark as nightfall.

At the port of entry and highway on the Mexican side of the bridge, a border guard stopped us. He tapped on the window of the driver's side of the car.

Don't move, Pearl, Corazón said to me. Don't even breathe.

I have the money here, Corazón said as Ray stopped the car and turned off the engine.

Yellow Pages *Branchenbuch*

Juárez-Lincoln Bridge bridge that connects the USA and Mexico over the Rio Grande

Ray pushed the switch and listened as the power windowpane went down on the driver's side. I also heard the rustle of paper as he handed the guard a large, yellow manila envelope.

Some words were said in Spanish and then Ray turned on the engine and steered the car toward the highway.

As we drove away, we left the storm behind us in the United States of America.

Don't be afraid, Corazón said. Ray likes to drive really fast. He doesn't care about speed limits.

As the gauge on the speedometer moved up, the car was lit with sunlight. Corazón rolled down the window and a warm breeze blew into the car.

The piece of sky turned blue as Ray picked up speed, going faster and faster into Mexico.

I lay among the guns and knew I lay among the deaths that had been and the deaths that were coming.

The sunlight and speed made me sleepy and I eased into the cradle-bag that held my body.

In my daydream I lay among skeletons, as gun parts were long femurs and ribs and short ulnas and ribs like the images in X-rays, X-rays of pieces of broken bodies broken, and I smelled gunpowder and maybe I smelled rust and blood and blood and rust. And the souls of animals and the souls of people were all around me and I heard a song of praise. Applause. I heard *Pearl, Pearl, Pearl* in congratulation.

switch *Schalter*

gauge [geɪdʒ] *Anzeige, Zeiger*

to ease into to relax

cradle [ˈkreɪdəl] *Wiege*

femur *Oberschenkelknochen*
ulna *Elle (Unterarmknochen)*
X-ray *Röntgenbild*

Additional texts

About the Author – Jennifer Clement

Jennifer Clement (* 1960) was born in Greenwich, Connecticut, USA, but moved with her family to Mexico City, Mexico, in 1961, where she grew up. Clement studied Literature and Anthropology at the New York University and in Paris. She also holds a Master of Arts (M.A.) degree from the University of Southern Maine. Jennifer Clement has two children and lives in Mexico City.

Professional career

From 2009 to 2019 Clement was the president of PEN Mexico, where she supported the work and safety of journalists and helped change the law, making the killing of journalists a federal crime.

In 2015, Jennifer Clement was the first woman to be elected President of PEN International, where she continues to fight for the right of free speech in the name of authors internationally.

PEN a worldwide association of writers, founded in 1927 to promote freedom of expression

Literary work

In 2000, Clement's first book, *Widow Basquiat*, was published, a memoir to the painter Jean Michel Basquiat, who died in 1988 from an overuse of drugs.

So far, Clement has published four novels and several volumes of poetry.

- **A True Story Based on Lies** (2001) – a novel set in Mexico, about class discrimination, male oppression and female servitude.
- **The Poison That Fascinates** (2008) – a novel about murderous Mexican women who are 'bewitched'; Hollywood actress Whoopi Goldberg bought the film rights.
- **Prayers for the Stolen** (2014) – a novel about the trafficking and sexual abuse of young women by drug dealers and their networks in Mexico.
- **Gun Love** (2017)

servitude the state of being under the control of sb. else and having no freedom

trafficking the act of buying or selling people

Among the many **awards** Jennifer Clement received are:

- The Guggenheim Fellowship (2016)
- PEN/Faulkner Award for Fiction (2015)
- The Sara Curry Humanitarian Award (2014)

Jennifer Clement was chosen 'writer in residence' in

- Berlin (2004) by the Goethe Institute and Literarisches Colloquium

- Belgium (2007) by PEN Vlaanderen, Antwerp
- Lynchburg College, Virginia, USA.

Original contribution by Iris Edelbrock

James Baldwin

You Don't Need Numbers; You Need Passion

James Baldwin (1924 – 1987) was an African-American poet, writer, playwright and civil rights activist. Growing up in a poor family in Harlem, he had to deal with racism and social injustice. In 1963, Baldwin participated in the famous March to Washington in support of Martin Luther King's campaign.

Being gay, Baldwin moved to France in 1970 to avoid persecution and prejudice. Baldwin was befriended by and inspired many famous actors, writers and activists like Nina Simone, Marlon Brando and Martin Luther King.

The 2016 documentary *I'm Not Your Negro*, which the excerpt is taken from, was based on Baldwin's unfinished manuscript *Remember This House*.

What can we do?
Well, I'm tired ...
I don't know how it will come about.
I know that no matter how it comes about,
it will be bloody;
it will be hard.
I still believe that we can do with this country
something that has not been done before.
We are misled here because we think of numbers.

You don't need numbers; you need passion.

And this is proven by the history of the world.
The tragedy is that most of the people
who say they care about it do not care.
What they care about is their safety and their profits.
The American way of life has failed –
to make people happier or make them better.
We do not want to admit this,
and we do not admit it.
We persist in believing that
the empty and criminal among our children
are the result of some miscalculation
in the formula that can be corrected;
that the bottomless and aimless hostility

to come about (*phr. v.*) to happen, to start to happen

to persist to continue doing sth. in a determined, but often unreasonable way; *auf etw. bestehen, beharren*

bottomless without limit or end
hostility *Feindseligkeit*

which makes our cities among the most dangerous
in the world is created, and felt,
by a handful of aberrants;
that the lack, yawning everywhere in this country,
of passionate conviction, of personal authority,
proves our rather appealing tendency
to be gregarious and democratic.

To look around the United States today
is enough to make prophets and angels weep.
This is not the land of the free;
it is only very unwillingly and sporadically
the home of the brave.

aberrant [ə'berənt] (*fml.*) sb. who is different from what is typical or usual, esp. in an unacceptable way; abnormal
to yawn *gähnen*
conviction *Überzeugung*
gregarious liking to be with other people
to weep (*lit.*) to cry
sporadically sometimes, not regularly or continuously

I Am Not Your Negro by James Baldwin and Raoul Peck. Based on the film *I Am Not Your Negro* © 2016 by Velvet Film, Inc. and Velvet Film SAS. Penguin, New York 2017, pp. 95ff.

Team Trace

14 Facts: Understanding Gun Violence in America

01 – There's not really a federal ban on gun-violence research. It's a common refrain among gun-reform advocates, lawmakers, and the press: The federal government has explicitly banned research on gun violence. But that's not what the law says. In 1996, at the behest of the National Rifle Association, Representative Jay Dickey of Arkansas inserted a measure into an appropriations bill that barred the Centers for Disease Control and Prevention from funding research to "advocate or promote gun control." [...]

02 – There are more murders in Chicago each year than in New York and Los Angeles combined. But it isn't the deadliest large city in America. There is no American city more synonymous with gun violence than Chicago. Last year, the city recorded 762 homicides, and more than 3,000 shooting incidents — the most in more than two decades. [...]

03 – A woman is shot by her partner every 16 hours. At least 6,875 people in the U.S. were fatally shot by romantic partners between 2006 and 2014, an analysis by the Associated Press found. Eighty percent of those victims were women. We did the math: that works out to at least 554 women fatally shot by a current or former romantic partner during the nine years examined — or one every 16 hours. [...]

refrain a phrase that is often repeated
behest (*fml.*) *Antrag, Anfrage*
to insert to add sth.
measure *Maßnahme*
appropriations bill spending bill; a proposed law that allows the spending of government funds
homicide an act of murder

04 – Violent gun crime varies even more *within* American cities than *between* them. The homicide rate in New York City, which has plunged dramatically since the mid-1990s, approached historic lows in 2016, registering at 3.9 per 100,000 residents. Chicago's rate soared, to 28.6 per 100,000. [...]

05 – There's probably been a shooting near where you live. In collaboration with Slate, we mapped every reported incident of gun violence in America from June 13, 2015 to June 13, 2016. Our map shows that while shootings are disproportionately clustered in a handful of cities, almost no community in the country is completely free of gun violence. [...]

06 – The NRA is dominant at the state level. Over the last decade, the National Rifle Association has successfully pushed a host of state legislatures to roll back long-standing restrictions on guns. Across the country, laws have been enacted that allow firearms on college campuses and into churches and bars; in a dozen states, permits are no longer required to carry concealed handguns. One reason for these major shifts, which often don't enjoy widespread public support, is the NRA's influence over state lawmakers. [...]

07 – America has more guns than cars. And more gun stores than coffee shops. American gun ownership has radically changed in the past two decades, defined now by the sheer ubiquity of civilian-owned firearms. The National Firearms Survey, conducted by public health researchers at Harvard and Northeastern universities, was the first comprehensive measure of gun owners' habits and attitudes since 1994. It found that Americans own approximately 265 million firearms, an increase of 70 million since the last time such a survey was conducted. Most of that increase was due to a surge in the popularity of handguns, as more Americans buy weapons primarily to defend themselves from others rather than to hunt. A gun-hungry America is served by approximately 60,000 licensed gun retailers – almost double the number of coffee shops in the country. [...]

to plunge to move or fall suddenly
to approach here: to reach
to soar to rise very quickly to a high level
Slate a US online magazine of news, politics, technology and culture, owned by *The Washington Post*
to map sth. to list according to location
disproportionally well above average
to cluster to happen a lot in the same small area
host a large number
to roll back to get rid of
permit an official document that allows you to do sth.
concealed kept hidden or where it cannot easily be seen
ubiquity [juːˈbɪkwəti] (*fml.*) the fact that sb./sth. seems to be everywhere
to conduct to organize sth.
comprehensive complete
surge a sudden and great increase

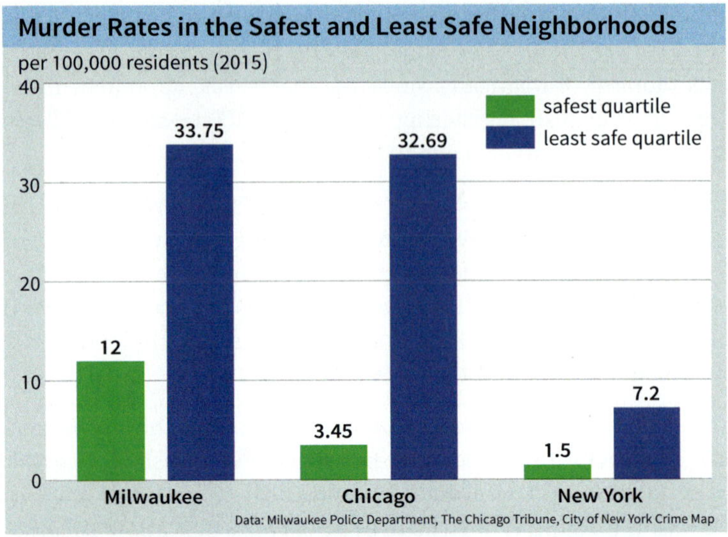

quartile in statistics, one of four equal parts that a set of figures is divided into, in order of size, amount, value, etc.

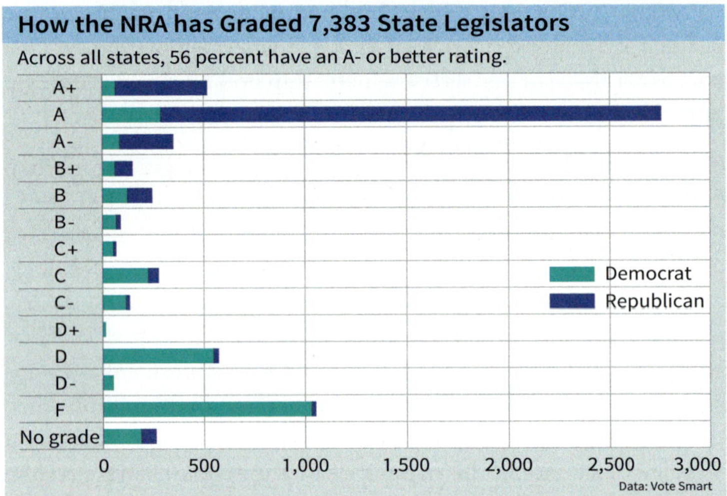

to grade to separate people or things into different levels of quality, size, importance, etc.
legislator *Gesetzesmacher*

08 – Gun suicides are on the rise in 21 states. Two-thirds of the 33,000 annual gun deaths in America are suicides. And rates are increasing. Between 1991 and 2015, the gun-suicide rate rose in 21 states. The greatest leaps were in Alaska and North Dakota, with notable jumps in Oklahoma, Delaware, and New Hampshire. Research suggests a connection between a state's gun regulations and its suicide rate, according to a study by the Boston University School of Public Health. [...]

leap a big change or increase
notable considerable

09 – Gun thefts appear to be the rise, and cars are especially hot targets. Cars, especially in states with relaxed gun laws, have become prime targets for thieves looking for guns. The Trace gathered statistics from more than 100 major cities that collectively tallied at least 57,700 firearms reported swiped from vehicles be-

the Trace an independent US news agency reporting on and campaigning against gun violence
to tally to count or calculate sth.
to swipe sth. from sth. (*infml.*) to steal

tween 2006 and 2015. San Antonio, Texas, and Atlanta each counted more than 850 guns stolen from vehicles in 2015 alone. […]

10 – The NRA is so much more than just a gun-rights organization. Over the last seven years, the NRA's core purpose has broadened considerably. While still preoccupied with gun rights, the NRA has evolved into a de facto organ of the Republican Party, devoting a huge portion of its vast monetary resources to preserving and expanding GOP power. In 2016 alone, it spent over $30 million to help elect Donald Trump – more than any other outside group – and another $20 million on Republican Senate candidates. […]

pre-occupied thinking or worrying about sth. too much
to evolve to develop gradually
to devote sth. to sb. (*phr. v.*) *etw. voll und ganz jdm./etw. widmen*
GOP Grand Old Party = The Republican Party

11 – Magazine capacity may be the best indicator of a gun's lethality. In some cities where shootings have spiked over the past few years, like Baltimore, police are noticing a disturbing trend: firearms turning up at crime scenes are equipped with larger and larger magazines. Using a gun with a high-capacity magazine enables shooters to fire more rounds before stopping to reload. […] According to one study, assault weapons and/or guns equipped with high-capacity magazines were used in 64 percent of mass shootings from 1984 to 2016, and killed more than three times the number of people than those shootings committed with smaller magazines. […]

lethality deadliness
to spike to rise to a higher amount
assault weapon *Sturmgewehr*

12 – The biggest background check loophole looks like it's shrinking. Earlier this year, researchers updated one of the most divisive statistics in the gun debate: the percentage of gun owners who purchase weapons without undergoing a background check. They found that just 22 percent of owners who acquired a gun within the past two years reported doing so without screening. […]

loophole *Gesetzeslücke; Schlupfloch*
screening a test or examination to discover if there is anything wrong with sb.

13 – A child dies in an accidental shooting every week. Young children shoot themselves or each other with alarming frequency. On average, one child under the age of 12 dies every week from an accident involving a gun. Typically, the firearm belongs to an adult, who left his or her firearm unsecured and readily accessible. Yet only 14 states have laws that require adults to store their weapons in such a way that children cannot access them. The NRA is adamantly opposed to safe-storage bills, and lobbies extensively against them. Between 2012 and 2016, 11 states tried to create safe-storage laws, and none were successful. […]

readily easily
adamant unwilling to change one's opinion or position
bill *Gesetzesvorlage*
to lobby to try to persuade an elected official to take a particular action or change a law

14 – For every person shot and killed, two more are wounded by guns and survive. Each day, approximately 93 Americans die

to obscure to prevent sth. from being seen
toll deaths, suffering

nonfatal sth. that does not cause death

from a gunshot wound. That figure, while alarming, obscures the true toll of gun violence. Guns wound significantly more people than they kill. In 2014, there were an estimated 33,000 gun deaths, and 81,000 nonfatal gun injuries.

About The Trace

The Trace is an independent, nonprofit news organization dedicated to expanding coverage of guns in the United States. We believe that our country's epidemic rates of firearm-related violence are coupled with a second problem: a shortage of information about the issue at large.

https://www.thetrace.org/2017/06/14-facts-gun-violence-america, 19 June 2017 [09.03.2019]

Joe Eskenazi

How US Cities Are Changing for Runaway Kids

WTF (*abbr., sl.*) What the fuck!
to retrieve to find and bring back sth.
to bolt to move very fast, esp. out of fear
to cower to lower your head and body in fear, often while moving backwards
luminescent [ˌlu:mɪˈnesənt] shining and reflecting light
all but inhale (*infml.*) *verschlingen*

a bit of column A and a bit of column B (*infml.*) a combination of two lots of factors

stretch a long period of time

The first thing Zach Hicks did after he was run over in Roanoke, Virginia, was to write a Facebook post. He kept it simple: "I just got ran over by a truck." The first commenter was his mother, hundreds of miles away in the midwest, who also kept it simple: "WTF!?!?!?!?"

He was retrieving a dog, Sobaka, that he'd been given by a band of Hell's Angels. The dog had bolted and was cowering beneath an 18-wheeler truck. Against his better judgment, Hicks crawled under to pull Sobaka out, and was hit. [...]

Hicks is joined by a dozen tattooed and pierced young men and women wearing luminescent orange vests. They smoke, sip Gatorade, and all but inhale three donated pizzas between shifts sweeping the pavement and wiping graffiti off the walls. Some of these young people ran away from home, some were abandoned, and some experienced a bit of column A and a bit of column B. Christian Calinsky, the founder of Taking it to the Streets, a work and housing programme for young homeless people, considers it largely a difference without a distinction – in his mind they simply "left home".

"They're both on the same playing field, man. I really can't distinguish," says Calinksy, 44, a former runaway who was homeless for large stretches between ages 12 and 34. "All their traumas are the same in my mind. But I don't see people as their trauma. I see them as their potential."

Hicks, 22, has plenty of both. He sports a beard like a rhododendron bush and a rugby player's build. He has piercing blue eyes, a ready smile, and the phrase “25¢ Jokes” tattooed across his knuckles. “That’s how I make my bread when I’m on the road. And it’s five for a dollar; when you buy in bulk you get the extra joke.” His story is instructive of the modern nature of runaways in the US. Hicks grew up in the economically depressed, dope-saturated Pacific Northwest. He shows me his ID; yes, he really was born in 1995. “Mum was around bikers,” he says. “I grew up in a double-wide trailer and she ran meth for bandits. She had me and stopped – but we still had all our connections to the brotherhood.”

He says his father would take him away as a toddler, only to mistreat him. After interventions by Child Protective Services, he ended up back in his mother’s custody. Before too long, Hicks says, “I got into some bad shit.” He burgled the medical marijuana outfit, making off with four pounds of pot; the next time he tried it, he found himself with a gun in his face.

After several years at a facility for at-risk youth in rural eastern Oregon, he was placed with an older family member “who had started smoking meth” and was living in a “backwoods, hickerbilly town where the only things to do are smoke meth, smoke weed or drive a big truck around in circles”.

Like many young men and women across the country, he says he had no choice but to leave. He ended up in a fetid squat, first rooming with meth friends and then, after a police raid, sleeping alongside them in a cave in Bend, Oregon. There, high and morbidly curious, they set his sleeping bag ablaze. […]

And so Hicks ran away to a new life. He hitched three rides over five days from Virginia to San Diego. “If you get in the wrong car or piss off the wrong person, you’re dead. One false move and you’re done.” And then he smiles. “But it is fun, man.” […]

Kids have always run away from home. The places they flee to, however, are changing. Today’s runaways are finding themselves adrift in much costlier cities, where even fully employed and well-educated people are finding it increasingly difficult to scrape by. In San Francisco – a city with a $10bn municipal budget and a population of only around 870,000 – one of every 25 public school students is homeless. That’s about one in every classroom. […]

It’s hard to know for certain whether there are more or fewer runaways now. A federally funded national tally is due this year – the first since a Department of Justice survey back in 1999, which estimated that 1.68 million young Americans had experienced a “runaway/throwaway episode”. […]

Findlay [of the National Center for Missing & Exploited Children (NCMEC)] confirms that of the more than 18,500 endangered runaways who reported to his organisation in 2016, one in six was deemed a likely victim of child sex trafficking. Of those, sev-

in bulk in large amounts
instructive informative
dope-saturated filled to the fullest extent possible with marijuana or any other kind of drug
to run sth. to sell sth.
meth (*abbr., infml.*) crystal meth, methamphetamine
toddler a young child
custody *Aufsicht, Obhut*
to burgle *einbrechen, ausrauben*
to make off with sth. (*phr. v.*) to steal sth.
hickerbilly (*Midwestern slang term, disapproving*) rural and backward
fetid (*fml.*) smelling extremely bad and stale
squat the act of living in an empty building without the permission of the owner
morbidly too interested in unpleasant subjects, esp. death
ablaze burning very strongly
to piss sb. off (*sl.*) to annoy sb.
adrift without a clear purpose in life
costly expensive
to scrape by (*phr. v.*) to have only enough money to pay for the basic things you need
tally a count of a number of things
to deem (*fml.*) to consider sth.
sex trafficking the act of buying or selling people and force them to have sex as work

en out of eight were in the care of social services before they went missing.

LGBT (*abbr.*) lesbian, gay, bisexual and transgender
foster child *Pflegekind*

As well as LGBT youth, foster children are also heavily overrepresented among the runaway population. In San Francisco, one in every four homeless people under 25 is a former foster child; and one in every five foster children is expected to experience homelessness within four years of leaving the programme. [...]

to allot *zuteilen, zuweisen*

In San Francisco, nearly a quarter of a billion dollars is allotted annually to combat homelessness, but only 8% of it is directed toward young people – despite 21% of the city's tallied homeless being younger than 24. [...]

intervention *Eingreifen*
to trigger to cause sth. to start
truancy *Schulschwänzen*
substance abuse *Drogenmissbrauch*

In Los Angeles County, interventions are triggered when children exhibit certain warning signs, such as chronic truancy or substance abuse. On the federal level, Bardine's organisation has created a comprehensive System to End Youth and Young Adult Homelessness broken down into prevention services, early and crisis intervention services, long-term services and after-care services.

to minister to take care of sb.

"We have to be looking earlier," says Doug Styles, the executive director of Huckleberry Youth Programs, a San Francisco-based agency ministering to young homeless people that was formed in 1967. More than nine in 10 young people who show up at Styles' door are eventually reunited with their families. But the real trick would be preventing that trip in the first place, he says. "We can probably identify some profiles of people likely to become homeless. We should be working with them earlier on. We should be working with school systems." [...]

https://www.theguardian.com/cities/2017/oct/09/one-false-move-and-youre-done-how-us-cities-are-changing-for-runaway-kids, 9 October 2017 [16.03.2019]

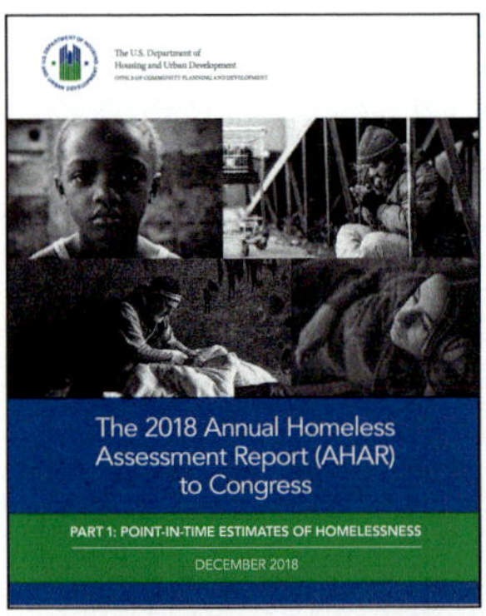

point-in-time at a particular moment
guardian a person who has the legal right and responsibility of taking care of sb. who cannot take care of himself or herself, such as a child

The Annual Homeless Assessment Report (AHAR) to Congress (2018)

Every year, the US Department of Housing and Urban Development (HUD) compiles a report of sheltered and unsheltered urban populations in the USA. The data are based on so-called "single-night" as well as "point-in-time" counts of homeless people and also include information on the demographic characteristics of homeless persons such as age, gender, and familial status.

In recent years, HUD has expanded Point-in-Time (PIT) count data collection to include information on the number of young adults and children who are experiencing homelessness without a parent or guardian present. Unaccompanied youth are people under the age of 25 who are not accompanied by a parent or guardian and are not a parent presenting with or sleeping in the same place as his or her children. [...]

Estimates of Unaccompanied Homeless Youth
By Age and Sheltered Status, 2018

	Total Unaccompanied Homeless Youth		Sheltered Unaccompanied Youth		Unsheltered Unaccompanied Youth	
	#	%	#	%	#	%
Total Homeless Youth (under 25)	**36,361**	**100.0%**	**18,011**	**100.0%**	**18,350**	**100.0%**
Homeless Youth (under 18)	4,093	11.3%	2,014	11.2%	2,079	11.3%
Homeless Youth (18–24)	32,268	88.7%	15,997	88.8%	16,271	88.7%

Demographic Characteristics of Unaccompanied Youth

- Just under 40 percent of unaccompanied youth experiencing homelessness were women or girls (38%), a higher percentage than of all individuals experiencing homelessness (28%). One-third of unaccompanied youth staying in unsheltered locations were female, compared to just over one-quarter of all unsheltered individuals (27%).
- Youth identifying as transgender accounted for approximately one percent of the unaccompanied youth population, regardless of sheltered status. Meanwhile, although an extremely small share of the overall unaccompanied youth population, people who did not identify as male, female, or transgender comprised a higher share of the sheltered population than the unsheltered population (2% compared to 1%).
- African Americans comprised a larger share of the sheltered unaccompanied youth population than the unsheltered population. African American unaccompanied youth accounted for a slightly larger share of the sheltered population than did all African American individuals (44% compared to 42%) and a lower percentage of unsheltered unaccompanied youth than all individuals (24% compared to 27%).
- Almost one-quarter of unaccompanied homeless youth were Hispanic or Latino (24% or 8,887 people). The rate is higher among unsheltered unaccompanied youth (29% or 5,387 people). Unaccompanied youth were more likely to be Hispanic or Latino than all homeless individuals: 24% of unaccompanied homeless youth were Hispanic or Latino compared to 19% of all homeless individuals.

unsheltered *obdachlos, ungeschützt*

approximately about, roughly

to comprise (*fml.*) to consist of

to account for (*phr. v., fml.*) to form the total of sth.; *sich auf etw. belaufen*

- Nearly half of unaccompanied youth were white (49%), and about one-third (34%) were African American. Multiracial youth accounted for 10 percent of all unaccompanied homeless youth. Native American youth represented four percent of the unaccompanied homeless youth population, and Asian and Pacific Islander youth together accounted for the remaining five percent.

Estimates of Unaccompanied Homeless Youth By State, 2018

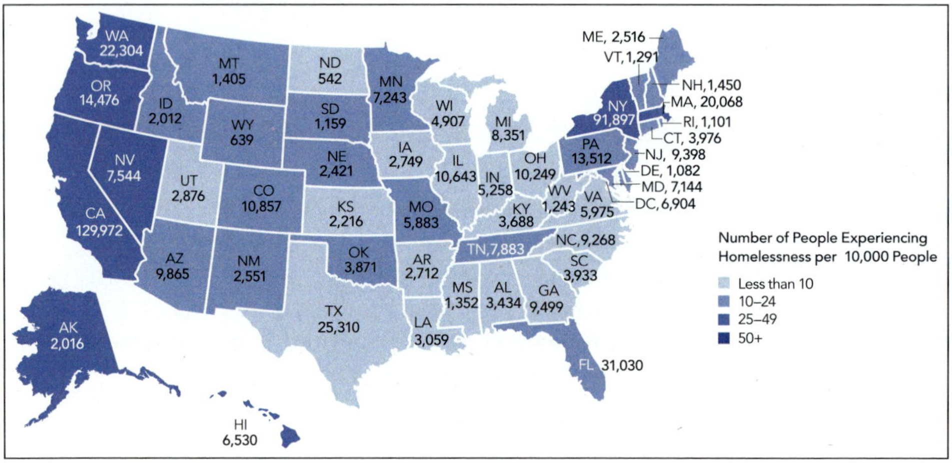

https://www.hudexchange.info/resources/documents/2018-AHAR-Part-1.pdf, pp. 46f. [16.03.2019]

Jeff Nesbit

Who Are We Preparing to Fight?

to gear up (*phr. v.*) to prepare for an activity or event

mayhem a situation in which there is little or no order or control

to cherish to love, protect and care for sth.

derision (*fml.*) action or statements showing that you think sb./sth. is ridiculous or of no value

to inflict to force sb. to experience sth. unpleasant

Something strange is happening in America. We're gearing up for a war with someone inside our own borders. But who is the enemy, exactly?

Mayhem and mass murders in public locations have become so commonplace now that it takes an *extraordinary* event to break through the fog of America's attention.

When the president of the United States [Obama], in his last year in office, cries real tears at the thought of more than a dozen school children dying because a mentally unstable individual with freely available, rapid-fire guns shoots them in their classrooms, the response by those who cherish their guns is derision.

When that same president – fed up with a Congress paralyzed by the ability of the NRA to inflict political damage to those who stray from freedom-to-carry gun laws – signals that he's going to issue executive orders on gun control, the result is ... the biggest jump in gun sales in years.

Smith & Wesson shares actually soared to their highest level in a decade after Obama announced new restrictions on gun sales. Consumers have rushed out in droves to buy guns, the company said. After domestic terrorists killed 14 people in San Bernardino, California some distributors ran out of some of their most popular guns. And the company, which makes a third of all revolvers owned in the United States, said its most recently quarterly sales would be much higher than earlier estimates. [...]

The United States has more guns in the hands of its citizens than anyplace on Earth. And yet, until President Obama issued a series of executive orders earlier this week, the federal government was barred from even researching the *impact* of the wholesale arming of America.

That change should at least tell us something about what's happening all around us as millions of Americans are armed with tens of millions of guns – unless Congress somehow figures out a way to block even this modest research effort.

But the bigger question still looms. Who, exactly, are we going to war with? Why do we need tens of millions of guns? Have we armed ourselves in every conceivable way so that we can shoot each other at the slightest provocation? What's next – gun turrets at street corners to keep the "outsiders" from entering our neighborhoods and communities?

Most people, including those in the media, don't realize that a majority of us support this effort to buy tens of millions of guns and arm ourselves to the teeth. People mistakenly believe that most Americans support gun control efforts. They don't. Gun control is a losing issue in America. [...]

"Gun violence has taken a heartbreaking toll on too many communities across the country. Over the past decade in America, more than 100,000 people have been killed as a result of gun violence – and millions more have been the victim of assaults, robberies, and other crimes involving a gun. Many of these crimes were committed by people who never should have been able to purchase a gun in the first place," said the White House fact sheet. "Over the same period, hundreds of thousands of other people in our communities committed suicide with a gun and nearly half a million people suffered other gun injuries. Hundreds of law enforcement officers have been shot to death protecting their communities. And too many children are killed or injured by firearms every year, often by accident," it said.

to stray from to move away from
to issue sth. to produce or provide sth. official
executive order (*US*) official instruction given by the president or a state governor
to soar to rise quickly to a high level
in droves in large numbers

to bar sb. from doing sth. to prevent sb. from doing sth
wholesale *im großen Stil, total*
arming *Bewaffnung, Aufrüstung*

to loom to appear, esp. when large or threatening

conceivable possible to imagine or to believe
turret *Geschützturm*

toll suffering, deaths or damage

assault violent attack

to purchase (*fml.*) to buy

law enforcement officer policeman

NRA (*abbr.*) National Rifle Association; US organization that advocates gun rights

to arm bewaffnen

Nowhere in this White House statement – despite the outcry from the NRA and other gun advocates – is even the semblance of a statement about whether it's a good idea or not for millions of Americans to own tens of millions of guns. It's nowhere to be found here, or anywhere else.

But it needs to be said. Something is wrong in America. We are arming ourselves, and preparing for war. But who is our enemy?

https://www.usnews.com/news/blogs/at-the-edge/articles/2016-01-08/americans-love-their-guns-but-why, 8 January 2016 [16.03.2019]

Susanne Mayer

Trump Country

ergreifend moving, touching

Halbwaise half-orphan

Panzer shield

Hillbilly Country a term for people living in rural, mountainous areas, esp. in the Appalachian region in the Eastern US

verhetzt filled with hatred

Lange ist nicht so ergreifend aus der amerikanischen Unterschicht erzählt worden wie in diesen beiden US-Romanen.

Zwei Halbwaisen, beide 14 Jahre alt. Pearl haust mit ihrer Mutter in einem Mercury Topaz Automatic, der auf platten Reifen in einem Trailerpark in Florida steht. Und Turtle heißt die andere, *turtle* wie Schildkröte, aber leider fehlt ihr, die allein mit einem gewalttätigen Vater auf einer Farm am Pazifik lebt, ein Panzer, unter dem sie Schutz finden könnte.

An diesen beiden Kinderleben entlang führen Jennifer Clement und Gabriel Tallent ihre Leser in eine Gefahrenzone, die aufmerksame Zeitgenossen als Hillbilly Country kennen, das große Reservoir der Abgehängten, der für den Amerikanischen Traum verlorenen Seelen, politisch betrachtet ein fanatisiertes, verhetztes Terrain: Trump Country. In den amerikanischen Wahlnächten leuchtet es auf in alarmierendem Rot. Bei Tage streifen Sozialwissenschaftler wie Arlie Russell Hochschild oder der Buchautor J. D. Vance durch die Ödnis, um zu erkunden, wie Menschen ticken, die am Rande von Industriebrachen und abgewrackten Träumen ihr Leben fristen, um zu verstehen, wieso sich in Amerika so viel Gewalt verdichtet. In den Nachrichten poppt diese Welt auf in Push-Meldungen über Massaker, gerade waren es wieder zwölf Tote, Barbesucher in Thousand Oaks, Kalifornien, vor ein paar Wochen 17 Schüler und Lehrer in der Marjory Stoneman Douglas High School in Florida und elf Tote in der Synagoge von Pittsburgh, letztes Jahr [2017] 58 Tote in Las Vegas – Statistiken des Horrors aus einem Land, wo auf 100 Einwohner 120,5 private Waffen kommen, was sich zu 393 Millionen addiert. Waffen spielen in diesen beiden Romanen ihre eisige Macht aus. […]

Als Pearls Mutter, die mit 17 schwanger wurde und die wie ihr Kind ein winziges träumerisches Wesen ist, sich einem als Cowboy daherkommenden Betrüger hingibt, sucht Pearl Wärme im Trailer einer Nachbarin. Dort sitzt sie, während ihre Mutter es mit ihrem Typen auf dem Rücksitz des Mercury treibt, und säubert Waffen, die ein Pfarrer unter dem Vorwand, die Welt sicherer zu machen, eingesammelt hat, um sie zu verticken. Mit ihrer Schülerschrift schreibt sie ordentliche Etiketten, eine typische Inventarliste lautet: „ein Smith&Wesson-M&P-Sturmgewehr, ein DPMS-Panther-Arms-Sturmgewehr, eine Smith&Wesson-Handfeuerwaffe, eine Llama-Handfeuerwaffe, eine Glock-Pistole, eine Smith&Wesson-Pistole, eine Taurus-Pistole, ein Del-Ton-Sturmgewehr, eine .40er-Kaliber-Halbautomatik-Pistole, eine .45er-Kaliber-Glock, eine Beretta-Pistole, eine Smith&Wesson-Halbautomatikpistole, eine Remington-Flinte, ein Bushmaster-XM15-Gewehr, ein .22er-Kaliber-Savage-Mark-II-Gewehr, eine Springfield-Armory-Halbautomatik-Handfeuerwaffe“ et cetera. Liest sich wie das Polizeiprotokoll einer Beschlagnahmung. Ist aber keines, ist auch kein Sachbuch. In diesem Roman, der den Titel *Gun Love* trägt, zeigt sich die überragende Leistung einer fiktionalen Erzählung in der Erfassung dieses Milieus. Mit der Auflistung der Waffen, gerade in der Exzessivität, verdichtet Jennifer Clement, 1960 in Connecticut geboren, mit Expertise, Wut und kaltem Hohn den bösen Hintergrund ihres Romans, der auf der Oberfläche leicht hingetupft im plappernden Jargon der kleinen Heldin daherkommt.

„Meine Mutter war eine Tasse Zucker, man konnte sie jederzeit ausleihen“, so süß geht es los, schon im ersten Satz. Und weiter und weiter, „sie ließ sich aufwühlen wie ein Milkshake, und immer von den falschen Leuten“. Kleine, atemlos hingepustete Sätze, Schlagertextsätze. Es ist der Endlos-Monolog eines Kindes,

Sozialwissenschaftler social scientist
Arlie Russell Hochschild (*1940) American sociologist and academic
J.D. Vance (*1984) American author and venture capitalist
Industriebrache brownfield site
verdichten to compress
Betrüger deceiver
verticken (*sl.*) to flog sth.
Schülerschrift childlike handwriting
Inventarliste inventory
Polizeiprotokoll police report
Sachbuch non-fiction book
Exzessivität excessiveness
Hohn scorn
hintupfen to dab
plappern to babble
hinpusten to blow gently

Kindmutter teenage mother
abgöttisch lieben to idolize sb.
Johnny Cash (1932 – 2009) American singer-songwriter; a country music icon with a deep, bass-baritone voice
Geraspel coarseness
Mattigkeit lassitude
Trivialität triviality
herauspurzeln to tumble out
Kitsch kitsch
Verlorenheit forlornness
Brache uncultivated land
Palimpsest palimsest; a very old text or document
albinoesk albino-like

das seine Kindmutter abgöttisch liebt und nicht verhindern kann, dass sie im Kugelhagel eines durchgeknallten Jungen zu Boden geht.

Den englischen *Guardian* hat das Buch an eine Mordballade von Johnny Cash erinnert, das ist natürlich Unsinn. Die Stimme, in der Jennifer Clement erzählt, hat nichts von diesem maskulinen Geraspel, da ist eher die süße Mattigkeit eines Teenies, der mühsam Haltung bewahrt und aus dem die Eindrücke und Gedanken und Trivialitäten nur so herauspurzeln. Clement, die schon ein Buch über in Mexiko gekidnappte Mädchen geschrieben hat, navigiert oft knapp am Kitsch vorbei, da ist eine Sentimentalität, die gelegentlich nervt, aber nun ja, dies ist wohl der Preis dafür, dass die Erzählung im Radius einer Schülerin verharrt. Ihre Mutter, fantasiert Pearl, lief in die tödlichen Kugeln, „als liefe sie an einem heißen Julitag in Florida in das Wasser einer Sprinkleranlage: mach mich nass mach mich nass erschieß mich erschieß mich" … Clement findet Bilder, in denen sich Verlorenheit apokalyptisch verdichtet – Kinderfüße, die über den von Krokodilen wimmelnden Brachen baumeln. Der mit Insektiziden ausgeräucherte Innenraum des Mercury, in dem sich Mutter und Tochter aneinanderschmiegen, zwei Gestrandete, wie wir sie von den Schwarz-Weiß-Fotos der Großen Depression der Dreißigerjahre kennen, Bildern von Dorothea Lange und anderen Fotografen, die durch diesen Text wie Archetypen auf einem alten Palimpsest aufscheinen. *God bless America!* […]

Übrigens mit dieser kleinen Zugabe an politischer Ironie, dass Pearl, dieses winzige, albinoesk wirkende Wesen, nur vor dem amerikanischen Unterschichtsdesaster gerettet werden kann, indem sie illegal die mexikanische Grenze überquert, ein Flüchtling aus dem Norden auf dem Weg in den Süden.

https://www.zeit.de/2018/48/us-romane-unterschicht-donald-trump-literatur, 21 November 2018, Nr. 48/2018 [16.03.2019]

Adele Peters

Can Manufactured Homes Help the Housing Crisis?

housing buildings for people to live in or the providing of places to live
proximity the state of being near sb./sth.

Tiny houses get all the attention, but mobile homes – despite the stigma – are already a huge part of the country's housing, and could have a bigger part to play.

For someone living in Sunnyvale, California, where the proximity to the headquarters of companies like Apple has helped push the cost of an average house to around $2 million, and a one-bedroom apartment now goes for more than $2,700 a month, the cheapest place to move might be a local mobile home park called Plaza del Rey.

That might not necessarily last: A hedge fund bought the park in 2015 and has been driving up rent for the land, which residents pay on top of the mortgage for their manufactured homes. (A home, on its own, can sell for as little as $150,000 for a two-bedroom, though space rent is now $2,000 a month.) But it's an example of a potential solution that can be overlooked in the conversation about affordable housing.

Manufactured homes are already somewhat common. A new report from Apartment List calculates that one in 18 Americans, or 17.7 million people, live in a manufactured home nationwide; the average monthly housing cost is $564, versus $1,057 for a typical house or apartment. In the 100 largest metro areas, people living in mobile homes spent around 40% less, on average, than others. At a time when the lowest-income families can't rent an affordable two-bedroom apartment anywhere in the country, and only 11% of low-income households get Section 8 support for housing, the report found that 1 in 10 people households living below the poverty line lives in a manufactured home.

"Mobile homes are kind of the last really cheap unsubsidized sorts of housing in most places," says Sydney Bennet, a senior research associate at Apartment List. They're particularly common in some areas – in Lake Havasu City, Arizona, for example, around 25% of the population lives in manufactured homes. Production swelled in the 1980s when the government cut funding for affordable housing. But new construction, despite the need, is slow. One challenge is zoning – communities heavily restrict where the homes can be installed, whether on single-family lots or in traditional mobile home parks.

"I think a lot of it really comes down to the stigma around living in a mobile or manufactured home," says Bennet. "I think there's still a lot of stereotypes about the communities who live in those areas ... and maybe policymakers don't consider it a desirable option." That's the case despite the fact that manufactured homes can, of course, be well-designed. [...]

Tiny houses, which can also be manufactured affordably but don't face the same stigma as traditional mobile homes, are slowly beginning to show up in new communities as well as individually on private land. (Most new manufactured homes are now built on private land rather than in communities, Goodman says.)

Manufactured homes, whether tiny or otherwise, could also help in fast-growing areas with a shortage of construction workers. "You have other areas that have lost their manufacturing and factory jobs who would love to have that kind of a plant," Bennet

hedge fund risikoreicher Investmentfond
to drive sth. up *etw. hochtreiben*
mortgage [ˈmɔːgɪdʒ] *Hypothek*

affordable not expensive

metro area commuter belt; densely populated areas surrounding cities

Section 8 support *Wohngeld*

unsubsidized *nicht-subventioniert*

to swell to increase

zoning the act of deciding what use an area should have
lot (*US*) an area of land

stigma *Schandmal*

desirable *wünschenswert*

plant factory

pre-fab (*infml.*) pre-fabricated; objects built from parts in a factory that can put together quickly
onsite happening in the place where sth. is needed

Fannie Mae FNMA Federal National Mortgage Association; a US government-sponsored company

re-emergence *Wiederauftauchen*
to sprout out *aus dem Boden schießen*
to stigmatize *brandmarken*

says. Pre-fab housing production, which uses factories to build the components of buildings and then constructs it onsite – unlike a manufactured home, which can essentially just roll into place – is also growing in response to construction shortages and to save costs. […]

But Fannie Mae is making financing less expensive, which may lead to more manufactured housing. Communities could also change zoning laws to further encourage new building. In some areas, one step might be new support for building tiny homes. "I think that if mobile homes are going to make a re-emergence in more expensive cities, I think we'd probably see it sprout out of the modular, tiny home movement because it is much less stigmatized," says Bennet.

https://www.fastcompany.com/40587942/can-manufactured-homes-help-the-housing-crisis, 22 June 2018 [16.03.2019]

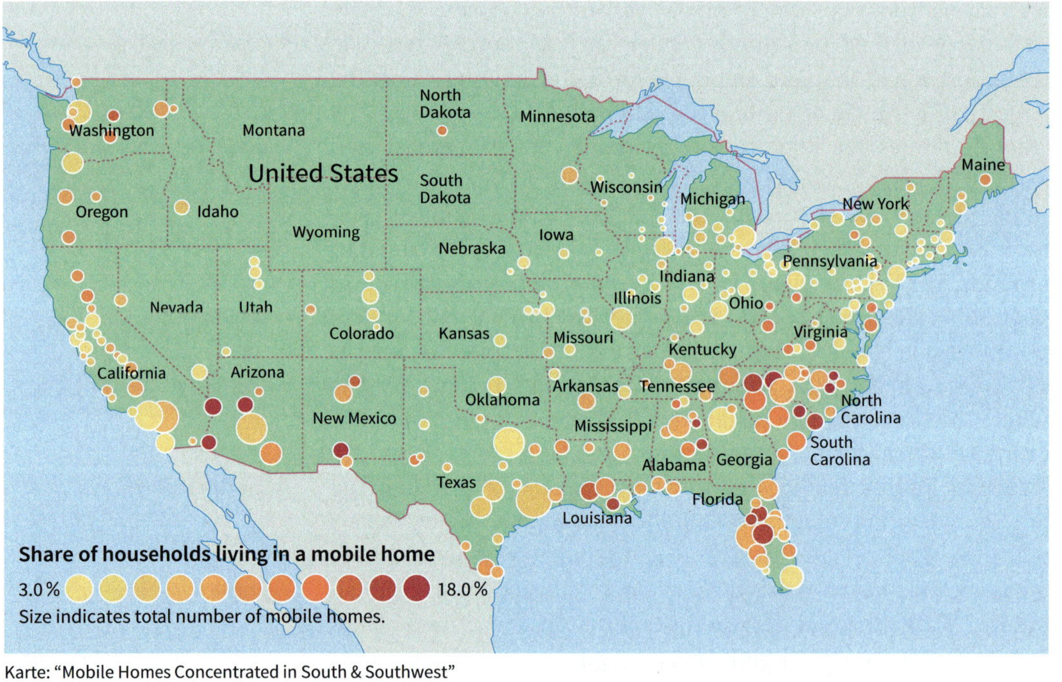

Karte: "Mobile Homes Concentrated in South & Southwest"

An interactive map can be found on www.apartmentlist.com/rentonomics/mobile-homes-affordability-crisis.

Skills & vocabulary

Structure and characteristic features of a novel

A novel is an **extended work of fiction** or **prose narrative**, which consists of **a connected sequence of events**. It can differ greatly in length and complexity.
Prose (= written or spoken language in its ordinary form, without metrical structure) is the most common form of language, because it applies to the natural flow and the grammatical structure of the speech.

Historical development

The word *novel* derives from the Italian word *novella* (= new).
Early examples of this literary genre are Giovanni Boccacio's *Decamerone* (1354), Geoffrey Chaucer's *The Canterbury Tales* (1386 – 1400), Miguel Cervantes' *Don Quixote* (1605/1615) and Christoffel von Grimmelshausen's *Simplicissimus Teutsch* (1666/68). Particularly Gutenberg's invention of the printing press in 1440, made the printing and publication of books a lot easier and available to a wider public.
In the **19th century**, famous English novelists included Charles Dickens (*Oliver Twist*, 1839) and Mary Shelley (*Frankenstein*, 1823); American writers of that time were e.g. Herman Melville (*Moby Dick*, 1851), Harriet Beecher Stowe (*Uncle Tom's Cabin*, 1852) and Mark Twain (*Tom Sawyer and Huckleberry Finn*, 1884).
Famous representatives of **modernism and post modernism** are F. Scott Fitzgerald (*The Great Gatsby*, 1925), Alfred Döblin (*Berlin Alexanderplatz*, 1929), John Steinbeck (*The Grapes of Wrath*, 1939) and Paul Auster (*New York Trilogy* (1985/86), *Moon Palace* (1989).
There are many **different types and styles of novels**, for example, romance, horror, mystery, satire, comedy, science fiction, fantasy, coming-of-age and gothic novels.
Famous and popular **coming-of-age novels** (*Entwicklungsroman*), depicting the development of the protagonist's mind and characters, commonly from childhood to maturity – and often through a spiritual crisis – include: J. D. Salinger's *The Catcher in the Rye* (1951), John Irving's *A Prayer for Owen Meany* (1989) and Stephen Chbosky's *The Perks of Being a Wallflower* (1999).

Characteristic features

In general, novels have a **fictitious but largely plausible content**, and tell **one or multiple stories** which usually are a **combination of prose and dialogue**.

As novels usually are quite long, they give room to the development of the plot and the character(s), presented in more or less complex situations and often in intertwined storylines which are connected and resolved in the course of the story.

intertwined *verwoben*

Narrator/writer/author

The **narrator of a novel often has a third-person omniscient** ("all knowing", "all-seeing") **point of view**, having insights into the characters' thoughts and emotions. However, other points of view or kinds of narrator are possible.

- The **first-person narrator** is a character of the story and has a limited point of view. He/she only reveals information from his/her perspective and often addresses the reader directly.
- Often, **interior monologue** or **stream of consciousness** are used to express his/her thoughts and feelings. As this type of narrator only has a limited insight into other characters' thoughts, he/she is often subjective and unreliable in his/her way of perceiving the events or characters. The stream of consciousness technique involves an **unbroken current** of feelings, impressions, fantasies, half-formed thoughts and awareness in which the narrator is independent in time.
- The **witness/observer narrator** is a character in a story, but usually takes a rather **objective point of view**.

current *strom*

Narration

There are several ways and techniques of narrating a novel that can be used.

- The narrator can vary the mode of presentation. He can use **panoramic presentation** in which the narrator tells the story in a condensed series of events, summarizing in a few sentences what can happen over a long period of time. In the **scenic presentation**, the narrator shows an event in detail as it occurs, using dialogue, depicting thoughts and emotions, describing a scene, etc.
- As a consequence, the **acting time** (*erzählte Zeit*) and **narrating time** (= reading time) can greatly differ and can be used so slow down action (element of **retardation**) or speeding up.
- Novels can be told **in retrospection**, i.e. a narrator talking about or reflecting and contemplating on an event in the past (e.g. in **flashbacks**), or there can be **foreshadowing**, i.e. there are hints given as to what might or will happen in the future.

to contemplate *betrachten, über etw. nachdenken*

Structure

- Novels are usually rather complex in their structure and development of the **plot** (= the sequence of events), often developing several storylines that are intertwined.
- The **plot** usually poses a problem which is resolved at the end or in the course of the novel. There can even be a "story within a

story" that can encompass a **long time span** and **different settings**.
- The **setting** (= time + place/social conditions) of novels can vary a great deal; it can be limited to a certain place and time but a novel can tell a story that takes place at a variety of places and can extend over centuries.
- Usually, novels begin with an **exposition**, which introduces the main character(s), the setting and background of the story, often leaving the reader with certain questions which evoke his/her curiosity and will then be answered in the course of the story.
- Often, novelists employ the so-called **"emotional extremes" technique**, i.e. exposing the characters to extreme situations such as happiness, sadness, painful or comic situations, and thus making the reader feel empathy with the characters' happiness and/or suffering.
- An important element of prose narrative is employing **elements of suspense** to hold on to the interest and anticipation of the reader.

Characters

The characters depicted in novels can have various backgrounds, depending on the plot and setting of the novel. There is no specific type of character that stands out. However, e.g. in a **coming-of-age novel**, the protagonist is typically a teenager or child, often a so-called "loner" or outsider who is suffering from an emotional or spiritual crisis caused by his/her parents, peers, etc. Sometimes, these characters experience extreme isolation or pressure, which makes them look at their environment from a new perspective.

Analysing a novel

When analysing a novel, it is important to pay attention to details. The following is a list of specific features of novels and questions related to them that will help you to examine and analyse central aspects of a novel.

Theme

Generally, a theme expresses the author's ideas and concerns about societal issues, loss, revenge, justice, etc.
- What is the novel's theme?
- How does the author implement the theme? E.g. through
  - images,
  - characters,
  - action,
  - direct/indirect statements.
- How does the central action and storyline of the novel reveal the theme?

Plot

A novel's storyline, the order of action and incidents, is referred to as the plot.

to evolve to develop gradually

- How does the plot evolve?
- (How) Does the author build suspense? For example by
  - slowly revealing events,
  - shifting between the past and present,
  - the use of memories,
  - the use of flashbacks or foreshadowing,
  - blurring memory.
- How do conflicts help develop the plot? For example by – things unsaid between characters – dramatic irony – anger – surprise – annoyance – (interior) monologue – dialogue – questions – commands – sentence length – hesitation – use of interruptions

to blur *etw. verschwimmen lassen*
annoyance *Verärgerung*
hesitation *Zögern*

Conflict

Conflict can be between two or more characters or simply one character (= **inner conflict**). Conflict can be verbal, physical or non-verbal (psychological).

- Where does the conflict lie?
- Is the conflict
  - between two characters,
  - within one character,
  - between a character and his/her surroundings?
- How is the conflict developed?
- (How) is the conflict resolved?
- Is the central conflict reinforced by other conflicts, e.g. between minor characters or in the setting?

Characters

Authors often use the characters to convey their messages or as a vehicle to convey their thoughts, values or criticism.
Characters bring stories to life.

- Does the character have a major or minor role in the central action of the novel ?
- What happens to the character throughout the novel?
- What changes does he/she undergo?
- What is the character's fate, his/her place in society?
- What are the character's strengths and weaknesses?
- How fully developed is/are the character(s)?
- (How) is the reader led to like or dislike the character?
- Do the characters convey their thoughts through monologues/ dialogue?

Structure

The structure of a novel reveals a lot about the author's intention and message.

- How is the novel structured?
- What is the effect and purpose of the structure?
- Is there a certain chronology or chain of events?
- How are leitmotif(s), climax, denouement, etc. placed within the novel? What impact does it have?
- Are there flashbacks, foreshadowing, inserted parts or omissions?
- Are there any elements of surprise?

Time

The use (or lack) of time is an important element for structuring a novel and for conveying a certain message to the reader.

- When is the novel set (past – present – future)?
- Are there different layers/levels/shifts of time?
- Are the characters preoccupied with time?

Symbolism/imagery

The use of symbols is most common in narrative texts and can be found in various elements, e.g.

  - objects and setting descriptions,
  - the characters' appearance, gestures and movement,
  - the use of leitmotifs,
  - the characters themselves.

- What images are used?
- How does the imagery help bring out the theme?

Setting

The setting (= time and place/social conditions) helps to give the reader orientation about where and when a certain action takes place.

- Does the setting have any particular significance?
- Does it add to the mood/theme of the novel? How?
- Does the setting change? How?
- What does the setting symbolize?

significance relevance, importance

Key lines

In some texts, certain key lines may reveal and convey the message of the novel.

- Are there specific lines that convey the central message/theme of the short story as a whole?
- Are certain lines repeated?
- What leitmotifs do these lines convey?
- What implications does the title of the novel have?

Characterizing a figure in literature

Fictional characters can be presented in a number of ways. In general, a character in a fictional text is developed through action, description, language and ways of speaking.

Types of characters

relevance within the text and characteristics	
• **protagonist** the main character around whom most of the work revolves	• **major characters** main characters who dominate the story
• **antagonist** the person who the protagonist is against; often the villain	• **minor characters** less important characters who interact with the main characters, thus helping to reveal the main characters' personalities, etc.
• **the modern hero** the average man/woman	• **dynamic/round character** three-dimensional, changing and developing personality, unique and different set of traits
• **the anti-hero** often dishonest, graceless or inept person who struggles in life; the loser	• **static/flat character** one-dimensional, unchanging, often stereotypical
• **the tragic hero** e.g. *Macbeth*; person who ends tragically as a result of his/her personal flaws	
• **romantic hero** a character with a strong will and personality who goes against established norms; often this figure experiences melancholy, isolation and unfulfilled and unhappy love	
• **the Hemingway hero** a character who has been to war, drinks too much, the loner, 'cowboy'	

Types of characterization in literature

- In a **direct characterization of a character** the author or one of the other characters **tells** the readers/audience what the character's personality is like.
- In an **indirect characterization** the author **shows/presents** the character through talking and acting, which reveals the character's personality. Indirect characterization can be achieved through:
  a) **Speech** (what does the character say, how does he/she communicate and interact with others?)
  b) **Thoughts** (what is revealed through the person's private thoughts, e.g. in a monologue, soliloquy, etc.?)

c) **Effect** on others/on the character (how does the person react/ respond to others? Does she/he have many relationships? How do others react to the person?)
d) **Actions** (what does the person do, how does he/she behave?)
e) **Looks** (appearance, body language, gestures, facial expressions, etc.)

Analysing the character of a figure in literature

In your analysis, focus on <u>how</u> a character does or says sth.

- How is the character's mood, feelings and way of thinking, his/her nature and beliefs reflected in his/her manner of speaking, choice of words and use of language in general?
- What additional devices help to flesh out a character to the reader?

Consider the following aspects and what they reveal about a character:

language register	formal, informal, slang, sociolect
choice of words	positive/negative emotive words, metaphorical language
imagery	use of simile, metaphor, personification
sentence structure	long or short sentences, repetition, rhetorical questions, exclamation, climax, antithesis
tone	ironic, sarcastic, upbeat, pessimistic, serious, light, nostalgic, humorous, pompous
sound effects	alliteration, onomatopoeia
action	• How does the character move and act? (standing, moving around, relaxed, hectic, etc.)
objects, clothing	• What are the characters holding and wearing? When?
setting	• Where does the character live? Are there changes? • What does the setting reveal about the character(s) in general (suburb, megacity, castle, prison, etc.)?
relationships / conversational behaviour	• Who has the most text/lines? • Who has the most turns (*Auftritte*)? • Who has the longest turns? • Who interrupts who? • Who is interrupted? • Who belongs or turns to whom? • Who initiates conversational exchanges and who responds? How? • Who uses speech acts like questioning, commanding, threatening and complaining? • Who uses speech acts like answering, agreeing, acceding (*zustimmen*), giving in and apologizing? • Who controls/changes the topic of talk? • Who uses 'title + surname' terms of address? • Who uses 'first-name' terms of address?

How to write a literary characterization

Step 1: Collect facts and clues given in the text and move from the outward features and characteristics to the inward nature of the character.

- **personal data** (name, age, sex, nationality)
- **outward appearance** (body, face, clothes, etc.)
- **attitudes/views** (thoughts, dreams, emotions)
- **behaviour** (toward other characters, actions)
- **relationships** (social background, family, friends)

Step 2: Draw your conclusion about the person's character and relate your findings to the text by referring to specific lines. Use the simple present tense for your characterization.

Step 3: Follow the 'introduction – main part – conclusion' pattern in your characterization: Write an introductory sentence that answers the w-questions.

Tip: Do not simply quote what a character says but **first** say what the character's feelings/mood are, **then** quote examples from the text for each separate aspect and explain what the choice of words suggests or how a certain action shows the character's emotions.

Vary the way you quote from the text by

- **referring** to an important part of the text (→ cf., cp.).
- **integrating a quotation** into your sentence, e.g. *April May dares Pearl to "steal" the toothbrush "and bring it to her" (p. 39, l. 12).*
- **using a full quotation**, e.g. *Corazón says that she has been looking around the house but "didn't find any cash either" (p. 117, ll. 39f.).*

- **note the abbreviations:**
  - one page or line: p. 8, l. 16
  - three or more pages or lines: pp. 4 – 7, ll. 16 – 22
  - the following page(s), line (s): f./ff. (e.g. pp. 20f. or ll. 15ff.)
- **omissions** of any kind are indicated by square brackets and three dots: [...]
- **remarks or changes from the original text** are indicated by square brackets:
  They [Leo and Helen] didn't wave back.

Vocabulary: Narrative texts and characters

narrative texts	
character	a) a person in a fictional story b) qualities of a person
conflict	a struggle between different forces that produces suspense
internal conflict	a struggle between two opposing views/values that takes place in a character's mind
(leit)motif	a theme/expression/object that recurs throughout the text and represents a certain person, situation or atmosphere
open ending	the conflict remains unsolved → the reader is left to reflect on possible resolutions
plot	the author's selection and structure of action as a set of events connected by cause and effect that are meant to create suspense
setting	place/social conditions and time of a story
suprise ending	a sudden and unexpected turn of fortune/action
suspense	a feeling of tension/expectation
tension	the emotional strain caused by a conflict
acting time	the time from the beginning to the end of an episode in a text, this is usually longer than the narrating time because the writer can describe the passing of years in just a sentence; *erzählte Zeit*
interior monologe	a technique used within the stream of consciousness; a special kind of scenic presentation, often not in chronological order
mode of presentation	the way the writer narrates events; *Darstellungsart*
panoramic presenta-tion	the narrator <u>tells</u> the story as a condensed series of events, summarizing in a few sentences what happens over a longer period of time
scenic presentation	the narrator <u>shows</u> an event in detail as it occurs, using dialogue, depicting thoughts and emotions, describing a scene, etc.
narrating time	(= reading time) the time it takes to relate an episode in a text; it depends on the mode of presentation; *Erzählzeit*
narrator	person who tells the story (***not*** the author!)
omniscient narrator	a narrator who seems to know everything (*allwissender/auktorialer Erzähler*)
point of view	the perspective from which the characters, topics and events are presented (***not*** the author!)
stream of conscious-ness	the presentation of experience through the mind of one character

characters/character traits			
active	*aktiv, tatkräftig*	**dull**	*schwerfällig*
adventurous	*unternehmensfreudig*	**easygoing**	*unbekümmert*
affectionate	*liebevoll, herzlich*	**energetic**	*kraftvoll*
alert	*munter, aufmerksam*	**faithful**	*treu*
ambitious	*ehrgeizig*	**fierce**	*kämpferisch*
annoyed	*unmutig, verärgert*	**gentle**	*leise, sanft, zart*
apologetic	*bedauernd*	**generous**	*großzügig*
arrogant	*arrogant*	**glamorous**	*glanzvoll, mondän*
attentive	*aufmerksam*	**gloomy**	*bedrückt*
bold	*kühn, gewagt*	**honest**	*ehrlich*
bossy	*rechthaberisch*	**ignorant**	*unwissend*
brainy	*gescheit*	**industrious**	*fleißig*
calm	*sanft, ruhig*	**mature**	*reif*
careless	*leichtsinnig*	**mysterious**	*geheimnisvoll*
cautious	*zurückhaltend*	**obnoxious**	*unausstehlich*
charming	*entzückend*	**pleasant**	*angenehm*
cheerful	*fröhlich, heiter*	**reliable**	*zuverlässig*
childish	*kindisch, naiv*	**responsible**	*verantwortlich*
clumsy	*tollpatschig*	**secretive**	*geheimniskrämerisch*
coarse	*grob(schlächtig)*	**skilful**	*geschickt, gewandt*
concerned	*besorgt*	**sly**	*verschlagen*
confident	*selbstbewusst*	**sneaky**	*heimtückisch*
courageous	*mutig*	**(stereo-)typical**	*stereotyp*
cowardly	*feige*	**stubborn**	*stur*
daring	*kühn, wagemutig*	**thoughtful**	*rücksichtsvoll*
decisive	*entscheidungsfreudig*	**trustworthy**	*vertrauenswürdig*
demanding	*fordernd*	**weak**	*schwach*
dependable	*verlässlich*	**wicked**	*böse, verschlagen*
determined	*entschlossen*	**worried**	*besorgt*

Acknowledgements

|alamy images, Abingdon/Oxfordshire: Granger Historical Picture Archive 149. |Cagle Cartoons, Santa Barbara, CA: Granlund, Dave 160. |Domke, Franz-Josef, Hannover: 152, 152, 164. |HUD Exchange, Washington: The U.S. Department of Housing and Urban Development: The 2018 Annual Homelessness Assessment Report (AHAR) to Congress 156, 158. |Suhrkamp Verlag AG, Berlin: © Brigitte Friedrich 148.